DESIRE OF NATIONS

The Magi, their Journey and the Child

Andrew Wheeler

Foreword by the Archbishop of Canterbury

a publication of Seismos Press Limited

SEISMOS PRESS

Desire of Nations

Author: Andrew Wheeler.

ISBN 9780993100147

BIC: HRCA; HRCG9; HRCM; HRCX7

Cover by He Qi, with thanks for his contribution in the whole of the book. www.heqiart.com

Artwork selected by Phil Simpson

Poems by Graham Kings

Desire of Nations
is a publication of Seismos Press,
a virtual imprint of bibleKiosk Limited
www.seismospress.com - info@seismospress.com

bibleKiosk Limited

bibleKiosk

www.biblekiosk.co.uk - info@biblekiosk.co.uk

Biblekiosk.co.uk is powered by gContentmanager, a service of Snowfall4POD Digital Limited

Table of Contents

FOREWORD

The headlines sound only too familiar: the sudden arrival of foreigners; strangers forced to make long journeys; political naïveté and power struggle; refugees fleeing terror; horrific violence and child abuse.

They may be familiar today, but they are also at the heart of the second chapter of the New Testament. Matthew writes of the journey of the Magi coming from the East. We probably think we know the story, from nativity plays, Christmas cards and Epiphany services. This book will cause you to think again - unlearning and relearning the significance of the narrative - as we plumb ever more deeply the depths of God's word.

Andrew Wheeler is an inspiring guide along that journey. Reading it is like being on a retreat with him. Heart speaks to heart. He draws on over 20 years' experience as a mission partner with the Church Mission Society. He served as a theological educator in Sudan (1977-86), and worked with Sudanese refugees in Egypt (1989-92) as well as from a base in Kenya (1992-2000). More recently he has been Mission Pastor at St Saviour's Church, Guildford and World Mission Advisor for the Diocese of Guildford.

Andrew has journeyed all over in search of the Magi: in churches and byways, by desert ways and in remote monasteries, as well as in the streets of Jerusalem and Bethlehem. He shares his re-reading of Matthew's story and we enter into it imaginatively, aided by the poetry of Graham Kings and art work from around the world collected by Phil Simpson. It is an upside-down story which makes us sit up and take notice afresh. Surprisingly, strangers from another faith come to worship the Christ Child despite (even because of?) dangerous power politics.

It is brought up-to-date with the report of the Millennium Peace Pilgrimage. In 2000 a few courageous pilgrims undertook a risky journey. They started in Ctesiphon on the Tigris River, twenty miles south of modern day Baghdad, and travelled about 1200 miles through Iraq, Syria and Jordan to Bethlehem.

I recommend you to read, to ponder… and to worship. You will not return disappointed.

Archbishop Justin

St. Matthew's Day 2015

ENDORSEMENT

Many years ago, before I came to faith myself in the child born King of the Jews, the one the Magi came to worship, I heard a preacher talk about them. He was at pains to convince us that these people were not *astrologers* so much as *astronomers*. He did so on the grounds, I suppose, that no-one as spiritually dubious as an astrologer could possibly be caught up in the purposes of God for the salvation of the whole world. I was unconvinced by his argument then, and am even less so now!

In this fascinating book Andy Wheeler (along with those who make their own distinctive contributions in word and image) helps us to recognise the strangeness of the Magi. We do not know where they came from (except for a vague 'the East'); we don't know their names; we don't know their number and we don't even know their gender. And yet, as we see, in all kinds of ways they have sharp contemporary relevance, and pose all sorts of questions for any of us who seek to worship the Christ-child in this day and age.

This is a work forged in mission, and from that it derives so much of its energy and wisdom. Church Mission Society's *raison d'être* has always been to cross cultures - and continents when needed – in following the call of Jesus and making him known. I'm delighted that Andy's journey in mission helps us to engage in such a stimulating way ourselves with the journey of the Magi, that we too may set out on mission as we seek to worship Christ.

And we should not be put off by the apparently dubious nature of the Magi. In that there is huge hope for us. The sweep of God's grace in Christ gathers up all sorts and conditions of people – even you and me. No-one is so far away that they too cannot come and worship Christ. In the end the strangeness of the Magi is of immense significance, because in Jesus we need be strangers no longer. As Christopher Idle so wonderfully puts it:

Jesus in you the lost are claimed
aliens are found, and known, and named.

May this book assure you too of just who you are in Christ, and inspire you afresh to serve him, worship him, and love him.

Philip Mounstephen

Executive Leader CMS

11th September 2015

AUTHOR'S PREFACE

JOURNEYING WITH THE MAGI

This journey with the Magi – I always assumed there were three of them - began some years ago. As my dissatisfaction grew with the way we told the Christmas story year by year, and the way we told the story of the Magi in particular, I somehow felt they would be the first to agree. They would understand my somewhat irritable and frustrated outbursts. If T S Eliot was right, they were quite capable of a good moan. They would have been eager to say what it was really like, and to point me to Matthew's succinct, unadorned narrative.

Well, I have journeyed in search of them, I have travelled with them. In the streets of Jerusalem and Bethlehem, in churches and byways, by desert way and in remote monasteries. Here is what I have learned from them. Here is my account of how, plodding along with them, I have learned about pilgrimage and worship, about the welcome, the cost and the exhilaration of the message that this Child has brought into the world. Thank you, Balthasar, Melchior and Caspar – let us at least this once give them names – I have learned so much.

Thank you, too, to others who have been on the journey with me – sometimes aware of the common search, sometimes not. In Bethlehem I am grateful to Emil and Elen Alqassis who gave me a home for a couple of weeks and shared with me the pain and hope of the Palestinian journey, to Dr Samy Awad, Director of the Holy Land Trust, and Dr Salim Munayir of the Musalaha Reconciliation Ministry.

And Dr Robin Wainwright who allowed me to see and profit from his accounts and photos of the re-enactment of the Magi's journey, the Reconciliation Pilgrimage of 2000 that ended in Manger Square, Bethlehem. Robin and Marianne Anker-Petersen, and David and Gita Jones provided me with shelter as later I pilgrimed my way to Iona and Sutherland.

Thank you, especially to Graham Kings, who set my mind off in all kinds of new directions and who, for this book, specially wrote the poems. And thanks also to Phil Simpson who helped me find my way through the thousands of mainly fanciful pictures of the Magi to find those that helped provoke thought and imagination. And together the three of us owe a huge debt to the Church Mission Society (CMS) in whose fellowship we all learned to cross frontiers, struggle like little children with language and culture, make countless friends, welcome a multitude of different expressions of Christian discipleship, and to see Christ in his variegated splendour in it all.

And to Sue, and our family, Clare and Nick, and Mark, for patience, understanding and encouragement. This is your book, and our book, uniquely.

Our church family, St Saviour's in Guildford, have encountered much of this adventure in sermons, conversations, retreats, when it was mostly a rummage room of bits and pieces. Their friendship and encouragement have been precious and deeply appreciated. I hope there are still fresh treasures here to excite and provoke. The places on the Isle of Wight to hide away and write are still remembered with gratitude.

And as the good news that the Magi encountered included them against every expectation, so my mind goes to so many friends, in Sudan, South Sudan, Egypt, Palestine, Eastern Africa, . . .even deepest Surrey, brothers and sisters, included, like me, against all likelihood in the Child.

And finally a suggestion as to how you might read the book. Most chapters begin with a reproduction of a work of art and a poem by Graham Kings, before the relevant verses of scripture. In general I do not comment at length on these. They are there for your reflection. It is intended that the art work, the poem and the scripture will get your mind and imagination moving in fresh directions before you start on the text of the chapter.

My love and gratitude to you all.

ANDY

Guildford, September 2015

PART 1: JOURNEY TO THE CHILD.

Mother and Child; Magdy William; Author's Picture

Journey of the Magi; Jan Richardson; Christmas Card;
http;//www.janrichardson.com/christmascards.html

CHAPTER 1.

SEEKING THE MAGI . . . AMIDST THE CLAMOUR OF BETHLEHEM AND A BRITISH CHRISTMAS

We know them well. . .or do we?

The Church of the Nativity in Bethlehem is a bewildering and ambiguous building – down at heel, seemingly unloved, but a centre of undoubted devotion. It is a major tourist attraction but one that evokes prayer and wonder; a place crying out for quiet, reverence and awe, yet overwhelmed by jostling crowds. The entrance to the church is barely one metre high, compelling everyone to bow their head and knee as they enter. Originally this was, apparently, to discourage Crusader knights from riding their chargers into church, but it was made even smaller in Ottoman and Turkish times. Whatever its origin, the tiny door is a parable and a reminder of the need for a humble spirit if you want to draw close to the Christ Child. Every time I enter the Church of the Nativity, this truth comes home to me afresh. We all need to come with humility and on bended knee, leaving the trappings of wealth and power behind if we are to encounter the Christ Child here.

If you want space and quiet in the Grotto – come early or late. I was there in mid-morning, the numbers, the heat and the irritation of the priests in charge all building up. I took my place in the queue in the south aisle. Because of on-going repairs, the Crusader paintings on the original Justinian pillars are covered up. Christmas bunting still adorns the lamps even though it is May. Candles and lamps burn before the icons.

Pilgrim crosses are gouged into the marble entrance as we arrive at the top of the steps down into the cave itself. We shuffle forward, pressed from behind, pressing those in front, feeling for the steps we cannot see for the crowd. The space inside, maybe 5 paces across, is packed with people, each trying to squeeze an opportunity to kneel in front of the arched opening, to kiss the silver star with its fourteen points, lay a hand on the rock where Christ was born, and say a prayer, before being urged on, up and out of the stifling heat into the relative calm of the church. Maybe even the air we breathe down here was breathed long before us by Crusader or Byzantine pilgrims.

I gave up on the struggle to reach the star, found my way to the back of the cave, and sat on a small stone bench. In front of me the heaving pilgrims, to the right a small chapel where Christ was supposedly laid after his birth, with an icon of my friends the Magi. What on earth was going on here, amidst the mayhem? Were the shepherds here somewhere? *Were the Magi?*

We know them instantly of course, wherever we met them - in a manger scene on our mantelpiece, on a greetings card, in a primary school play, the subject of a Christmas carol, on a Christmas advertising hoarding, or wherever across the world our paths might cross with theirs. Three of them - no more, no less - a camel apiece, one of them very probably black and African, crowns on their heads, flowing, exotic, colourful robes, gifts in hand. . . .

We'd recognise the setting as well. Either silhouetted on their camels against a night sky with a desert landscape illuminated by a huge star – or perhaps in a stable gathered around a new born baby with a crowded canvas of shepherds, sheep and farm animals, glittering gifts held aloft. They are the Three Kings, the Wise Men, the Magi. We know them well.

Or perhaps not as well as we thought. Sometimes I find within myself a sense of unease, of dissatisfaction. The story as we tell it year after year doesn't feel quite right. We speak of "incarnation", of the "Word made flesh", but this story has somehow lost its earthiness, its rootedness, a sense that it connects with real life. It seems so very far from Jesus thrashing out his vocation in the heat and hunger of the desert, or responding for long hours to the needy, the sick and the lost. It seems a long, long way from a baby's startled shout for breath, from the man who set his face like flint to go to Jerusalem to face murderous hostility, sweating with distress in the olive groves on the hillside outside Jerusalem, or surrendering to the brutality of the cross.

Somehow it no longer feels that this is how it was. It has gathered along the way too much glitter, romance, and midnight mystery. We have drawn in the children, but maybe closed the stable door on lots of other people. And then to learn that these exotic visitors, these Magi, may not, after all, have been Kings, or Wise Men, that we have redefined them, or that there may have been more or less than three of them, only deepens the mystery and puzzlement.

Revisited by the Magi. . .

For years I struggled with the strange mix that the Christmas season serves up for us: the odd marriage of a mid-winter festival and a religious celebration.

A strange stirring together of Father Christmas, parties, family gatherings and pantomimes with a good news message that, if it be true, raises huge questions about the surrounding extravagance. To live in both worlds simultaneously, the Winterval and the Christ-Mass, to accomplish both journeys, often left me tired and out of sorts (as well as over-fed and lethargic).

Then, if you belong to one of the more traditional churches, the Magi come back and visit you again in early January at the season called Epiphany. It was meeting the Magi again, on their return visit, that began the process of awakening me from my annual post-Christmas lethargy. For this is *Epiphany* – it is the time the Church sets aside to reflect more on what has just unfolded in the telling of the Christmas stories, and to look at the Big Picture. This is the story that begins to lay out for us the purpose of love of the Creator God, the God of Israel's history, for all people and for the whole of his Creation. And it is focused in this tiny Child. The Magi, wonderfully, now take centre stage, their story powerfully illustrating the larger meaning of the Christmas season, a meaning often obscured behind the sheer busyness and distraction of the season.

Epiphany – the "revealing of Christ to the nations" – with the arrival again of the Magi, became for me a new window into the story of Christmas, and how it can speak compellingly to us about what God is up to in our world. And it took me back to the Bible text where the story is told. It took me to Matthew's Gospel.

Whatever we might have done with the Christmas story, Matthew certainly cannot be accused of romanticising, fantasising, or of writing a script for a nativity play. He is beginning a story of immense import and consequence. This story will climax in its final extraordinary scene in which Jesus the Messiah, having suffered a bloody and humiliating death on a Roman gibbet, shatters the power of death and emerges triumphant and alive on the other side. In a final encounter with his followers Jesus gives them a commission, which has changed the course of human history, established a transformed and transforming community, and impacted the lives of many millions of people across the world and across two millennia. This commission sends them out to all nations to make more and more disciples of Jesus, baptized and taught in his Way. And he who was named Emmanuel – God with us – at the beginning of the Gospel (1:23) now takes up that title and promises that he will be with his new Gospel agents until the job is complete (28:20). And we stand in the contemporary realisation of that commission and that promise.

The man who tells this story has a very serious intent, and following an important introduction (which we will be looking at carefully), in chapter 2 launches into his first major narrative, a serious business in which the significance of what God is doing through the birth of Jesus begins to be uncovered. The Magi and the surrounding stories are his choice of how to introduce this and we run the risk of missing the overarching drive and purpose of the Gospel if we are not attentive to his carefully constructed story telling…

Bethlehem: Looking for the Magi

On sabbatical in May 2014, I gave time to visit and revisit the "holy sites", especially the Church of the Nativity in Manger Square. In particular I was searching for traces of the Magi.
I also drank a considerable amount of strong Turkish coffee at the Square Coffee Shop where I kept up with my journal writing.

Traces of the Shepherds are everywhere. They have gift shops and restaurants, churches and gardens. There are three sites – Catholic, Orthodox and Protestant – each known as the Shepherds Fields where the claim is that the "shepherds lay awatching their sheep" and angels appeared to announce the birth of the Messiah. Even with modern developments, each has its ancient feel and reward for the visitor. And each has its church or chapel. The Greek Orthodox Church has particularly beautiful icons and paintings completed in the 1970s.

Back in the centre of Bethlehem, Bethlehem Bible College, a crucial centre for training Christian leaders and keeping the flame of the Palestinian Church alight, has a magnificent sculpture standing three stories high of the angel announcement to the shepherds.

Traces of the Magi are more elusive. Dr Sami Awad heads the Holy Land Trust, a significant organisation working with reconciliation amongst the various communities of the Holy Land. His office is in the old town of Bethlehem in a restored building over the "canal" or viaduct that in Roman times was part of the water supply for Jerusalem. In 2000, at the height of the second Intifada, he had been part of a re-enactment of the

journey of the Magi from Ctesiphon on the Tigris River, through Iraq, Syria and Jordan to Bethlehem.
Imagine the complicated negotiations necessary to achieve such a journey! Preparations took eight years. Dr Sami finally rode a camel into Manger Square on Christmas Eve 2000. Suddenly the Christmas story of the Magi was springing to life for me as something contemporary, as well as ancient; a story that speaks to human issues across the centuries and is a challenge today. Maybe there would be further echoes.

I found those echoes at the Church of the Nativity, the traditional site of the birth of Jesus, and where both shepherds and Magi are remembered as visiting in adoration. Currently some work is being done on the roof and windows of the church, but generally the building is dilapidated and dirty and in urgent need of restoration. The thousands of visitors can hardly be aware of the remarkable building they are visiting.

The Church of the Nativity is the only Christian Church in Israel / Palestine that still survives from the early Christian era. It was one of the three churches built at the instruction of Emperor Constantine after 325, (the other two being the Church of the Holy Sepulchre, and a now vanished Church of the Ascension) following the visit of his mother Helena to Palestine. It was destroyed during the Samaritan revolt of 529 but rebuilt by the Emperor Justinian in the mid 6th century, and it is this building that essentially stands today.

It escaped destruction during the Persian invasion of 614, unlike the Church of the Holy Sepulchre and other ancient churches and monasteries. Reputedly, invading Persian troops, upon entering the church, found a mosaic portraying the visit of the Magi to the

Christ Child and showing them in Persian dress. So impressed was the Persian commander at this respectful representation of Persian people, or perhaps specifically of Zoroastrian priests – we don't know – that he commanded that the church be spared. The Bethlehem mosaic no longer exists but was probably not dissimilar to the Ravenna mosaic represented at the head of Chapter 2 of this book, which dates from the time of Justinian also. So the Magi, in the twists of Palestinian history, had had a role in the protection and preservation of this great church.

In front of me in the Grotto of the Nativity was an absolute tumult of languages and cultures. A fragile and anxious-looking elderly woman in a wheelchair was being manhandled down the steps in front of me by well-wishers. A sick nun on a stretcher was being inched forward by her fellow sisters. I could hear, or so I guessed, Arabic, Russian, Spanish, Portuguese, something Scandinavian and some occasional English. There were Christians from South India, the women in saris. There were Pakistani Christians, some I supposed to be Indonesians, Kenyans and Nigerians, and I think some Chinese. Many were softly singing praise and worship in their diverse languages, praying together, or even holding brief impromptu services. The whole world was here, in this tiny space, in the heat, packed shoulder to shoulder, doing their best to be present to the occasion, and present to Christ, to pray for loved ones, to rise above the stress, to be blessed. And they would carry the experience, the act of devotion, the prayer, the blessing back to the far corners of the world. It's easy to be sceptical about the pilgrim sites in the Holy Land – but here, day by day, thousands of people were trying to make the best of it, to strengthen faith, to pray, to be blessed, to be more faithful.

As I sat, my mind went to the first "foreigners" who knelt and worshipped Christ here, or not very far away. They doubtless spoke another language, were also trying to make sense of their strange experience, their long pilgrim journey and the Child before them. So they opened their treasures and brought out their gifts. They were the first in an immensely long line.

Adoration of the Magi; He Qi
www.heqiart.com

CHAPTER 2

DESIRE OF NATIONS! A DRAMA IN 3 ACTS

Matthew, chapter 2:

1 After Jesus was born in Bethlehem in Judea, during the time
of King Herod, Magi from the east came to Jerusalem **2** and
asked, "Where is the one who has been born king of the Jews?
We saw his star when it rose and have come to worship him."
3 When King Herod heard this he was disturbed, and all
Jerusalem with him. **4** When he had called together all the
people's chief priests and teachers of the law, he asked them
where the Messiah was to be born. **5** "In Bethlehem in Judea,"
they replied, "for this is what the prophet has written:

> **6** "'But you, Bethlehem, in the land of Judah,
> are by no means least among the rulers of Judah;
> for out of you will come a ruler
> who will shepherd my people Israel.'"

7 Then Herod called the Magi secretly and found out from
them the exact time the star had appeared. **8** He sent them to
Bethlehem and said, "Go and search carefully for the child. As
soon as you find him, report to me, so that I too may go and
worship him." **9** After they had heard the king, they went on
their way, and the star they had seen when it rose went ahead
of them until it stopped over the place where the child was.
10 When they saw the star, they were overjoyed. **11** On coming
to the house, they saw the child with his mother Mary, and they
bowed down and worshiped him. Then they opened their
treasures and presented him with gifts of gold, frankincense
and myrrh. **12** And having been warned in a dream not to go
back to Herod, they returned to their country by another route.

13 When they had gone, an angel of the Lord appeared to
Joseph in a dream. "Get up," he said, "take the child and his

mother and escape to Egypt. Stay there until I tell you, for
Herod is going to search for the child to kill him."
14 So he got up, took the child and his mother during the night
and left for Egypt, **15** where he stayed until the death of Herod.
And so was fulfilled what the Lord had said through the
prophet: "Out of Egypt I called my son." **16** When Herod
realized that he had been outwitted by the Magi, he was
furious, and he gave orders to kill all the boys in Bethlehem and
its vicinity who were two years old and under, in accordance
with the time he had learned from the Magi. **17** Then what was
said through the prophet Jeremiah was fulfilled:

18 "A voice is heard in Ramah,
weeping and great mourning
Rachel weeping for her children
and refusing to be comforted,
because they are no more."

19 After Herod died, an angel of the Lord appeared in a dream
to Joseph in Egypt **20** and said, "Get up, take the child and his
mother and go to the land of Israel, for those who were trying
to take the child's life are dead." **21** So he got up, took the child
and his mother and went to the land of Israel. **22** But when he
heard that Archelaus was reigning in Judea in place of his
father Herod, he was afraid to go there. Having been warned in
a dream, he withdrew to the district of Galilee, **23** and he went
and lived in a town called Nazareth. So was fulfilled what was
said through the prophets, that he would be called a Nazarene.

We hardly ever read the whole story. The Magi worship and bring their gifts to Christ, and shuffle off on their camels to their homes, and we move on to the next carol. In fact, in Matthew's telling, the visit of the Magi to the Child has catastrophic results – wild threats from a homicidal king, the desperate flight in the middle of the night by the Holy Family, and a bloody massacre of toddlers in Bethlehem by the king's troops. The story continues for a further 10 verses as the tragic tale unfolds. Why do we not read it? Often the only place where these shocking events make an entrance is in the singing of the hauntingly lovely but painful Coventry Carol:

> *Herod the king, in his raging,*
> *Charged he hath this day*
> *His men of might in his own sight*
> *All young children to slay.*

In so doing we sever Matthew's story in the middle and destroy its carefully developed balance and structure, and, very likely, much of its meaning. The story of the Magi, which takes up all of chapter 2 of Matthew's Gospel, is a Drama in Three Acts, succinctly told, emotionally restrained, but in which powerful and significant events are outlined.

The Still Centre – Worship and Offering

The second act of this drama, the middle, is its heart. Acts 1 and 3 are full of travel, of journeying, in urgency, haste, and even fear. Here at the centre of the story is peace and stillness as the Magi, star-led, having completed their journey of many miles and months, arrive at the house and bow before the Christ Child and his mother, offering precious gifts. Many artistic representations of this moment capture the wonder, the intimacy and the peacefulness of that moment.

The Journey to the Child – Magi, Call and Pilgrimage

Either side of this heart-stopping moment are the first and last Acts of the drama, full of journeying and upheaval, uncertainty, dreams and risk. The Magi are called by a star to search out the new born King of the Jews, and set out on a pilgrimage to find him. It is a journey that plunges them deep into religious and political machination and intrigue, possibly danger. Having achieved their goal and brought their gifts to the new King, they return home "by another route" to escape Herod's wrath, and so set in train the violent events of the second half of the story.

The Journey of the Child – Flight, Tragedy and Return

Like the first, the last Act of the drama is full of travel – now by the Child and his parents – to Egypt and safety from Herod's wrath. They escape but leave behind the bloody events in Bethlehem as Herod takes out his fear and frustration on the families of Bethlehem. The story concludes with the careful, cautious return, first to Judea and then to Nazareth in Galilee as Joseph tries to find a safe home for his young family.

There are further ways in which Matthew demonstrates his skill as a story-teller. Acts 1 and 3 frame and highlight the special wonder and significance of the family scene in Bethlehem. But each of these Acts also is constructed in a careful and effective way. In both cases there are, as it were, several "scenes" within the flow of the narrative.

In Act 1, the encounter with Herod broadens out as the Magi explain how they come to be on their quest. In this way we gain a glimpse into all that lies behind their sudden appearance in Jerusalem. In Act 3, we are first alerted to the grave danger confronting the family and the need to flee – and that draws us back to the grim events unfolding in Bethlehem.

So, the story is structured something like this. . . .

ACT 1
THE JOURNEY TO THE CHILD

- Magi, Star & Call
- The Pilgrimage
- Dangerous Encounters

ACT 2
WORSHIPPING THE CHILD

- Bowing the Knee
- Offering Treasures
- Returning Transformed

ACT 3
THE JOURNEY OF THE CHILD

- The Flight to Egypt
- The Massacre of the Bethlehem Children
- The Return to Nazareth

But what is it all about?

This outline will guide us through our reflection on the story of the Magi. It's a dramatic story, it's colourful, it stimulates the imagination. The three exotic strangers travelling to see the Child born to be king invite romantic realisation in song, or art or drama. But what is it all about? What is the key? Why does Matthew introduce these strange Magi? He is surely doing more than just recounting a story associated with the birth of Jesus. What significance is hidden within the story?

Already in chapter 1 of his Gospel, Matthew has been giving hints of what is afoot, of what the story of Jesus is about, what it is that inspires the small fellowships of believers in Jesus that were dotted around Palestine and for whom Matthew wrote.

Who is Jesus?

When Matthew wrote his Gospel in the middle of the first century, maybe 30, 40 or 50 years after the crucifixion and resurrection of Jesus, there were small communities of Jesus followers scattered over Palestine. These mainly consisted of Jews who had come to recognise Jesus as the Messiah, the fulfilment of the age long hopes of the Jewish people. These communities probably also included numbers of "Gentiles" – non-Jewish people, Greek- speaking probably, from various corners of the Mediterranean who were also intrigued by Jesus and had become his followers. These fellowships were still, in many areas, part of local Jewish society, though their devotion to Jesus and their inclusion of non-Jews created tension and debate, which would eventually lead to separation of the Christian groups from the Jewish communities and their synagogues.

Matthew is writing an account of the story of Jesus for Jewish neighbours who did not understand what Jesus meant to their Christian neighbours, and for the very new Jewish and Greek and Roman converts in the Christian assemblies. This first chapter of the Gospel addresses the question "Who is Jesus of Nazareth?" Indeed the whole Gospel addresses that very question.

A genealogy

For modern readers this is not the best way to start such a presentation – and I for one have never heard verses 1 to 17 of Chapter 1 read in any Christmas service! But to Jewish people of the first century – and indeed to many people in Africa and other parts of the world today – understanding the family tree is indeed crucial to understanding who someone is, and what their significance might be.

Roots

At the outset, Matthew lays out the central claims that will emerge. Jesus is:
<u>The Christ (or the Messiah) (1:1):</u> the claim of these new Jewish / Christian communities was that Jesus of Nazareth, an obscure village in Galilee, crucified by the Romans, unlikely as it may seem, is the Messiah, God's chosen and anointed answer to the hopes of the Jewish people.

<u>The Son of David (1:1):</u> The genealogy will demonstrate that through Joseph he is a descendent of David and so qualifies to be the new King in David's line, inheritor to all the covenant promises made to David.

Son of Abraham (1:1): It will also demonstrate a clear line back to Abraham, which of course all Jews would claim, though may not be able to demonstrate. But in the case of Jesus, Matthew is keen to demonstrate that ancestry is through David's line. This brought into the open the foundation charter of the Jewish people, and a central role of the Messiah – that God had promised to bless the people who came into being through Abraham's family, *and through them to bless the nations of the world!* This was the ground on which Gentile believers were accepted into the new Christian communities alongside Jews, and was a point of tension with the local synagogues.

Furthermore Jesus has some strange ancestors: The genealogical line that Matthew then lays out has some strange features. First it highlights that God is not the prisoner of human rules of inheritance when it comes to fulfilling his promises and purposes! The line lurches in some surprising directions. Jacob, known as the "deceiver", is chosen instead of his older brother Esau. Judah, Jacob's fourth born, carries the line forward rather than Reuben the first born. And there are other examples. This was not new to Jewish readers, but Matthew's purpose is to highlight the sovereign grace of God as he fulfils his plan.

Even more surprising and provoking is the way that Matthew highlights four women from the Old Testament, and then Mary, the mother of Jesus, in the list. The list of women is unsettling: *Tamar* (1:3) – who disguised herself as a prostitute and deceived her father in law, bearing him several children (the complex story is in Genesis 36), *Rahab* (1:5), the Jericho prostitute who protected the Israelite spies when they came to assess the land of Canaan for invasion (Joshua 2). *Ruth* (see the Book of Ruth) was not Jewish, but a Moabite, but became the grandmother of King

David. There is also some doubt about the innocence of her behaviour on the threshing floor towards her future husband Boaz! And *Bathsheba,* only described here as the *wife of Uriah* , who had an adulterous relationship with King David, and bore him Solomon, his eventual successor. All were familiar with scandal and marginalisation.

Again, Matthew is highlighting here the extraordinary unpredictability of the God of Israel. He is the God of the unpredictable and the irregular, using the most unlikely of people. He is the God of freedom, who brings his purposes to fruition in surprising ways –especially in the story of Jesus of Nazareth, the Messiah, the King of the Jews, the Saviour of the world. But as important as the "irregular" position of these four mothers in the line of Jesus, is the fact that they are all foreigners. Tamar and Rahab were Canaanites, Ruth was from Moab, and Bathsheba, at least by marriage, was a Hittite. This draws us back to the promises to Abraham, and the foundation "documents" of the people of Israel that through Abraham and his offspring all the people of the earth will be blessed. And here, along the way are repeated signs of God drawing "the nations" into the story, using them to carry the story forward. In this way, the tables are turned for a while. The foreigners, in the story by their role in the line of the Messiah, bless Israel by whom they will in the end be blessed. The genealogy may seem a dry document at first – but it has the most extraordinary themes running through it!

And Mary

It is these four women – not Israel's renowned matriarchs, Sarah, Rebekah, Rachel and Leah – who are the forerunners and the models for Mary. Like them, she is an outsider, not a foreigner, but a nobody chosen by the God "who lifts up the humble" (Mary's Song, Luke 1:52). Like them, to play her part in God's unfolding plan of salvation she had to endure scandal and abuse, derision and distain (1:19).

And, as we quickly realise when we reach 1:16, this is not even Mary's genealogy – it is Joseph's. Biologically, Jesus has no association with Joseph. How much an outsider Mary seems at this point! Jewish law in the first century gave an adopted son the same rights and indeed identity as a biological son. Jesus inherited his status as son of David, son of Abraham, as an adopted son of Joseph.

And the promise to Abraham, foreshadowed in the four foreign women in the ancestral line of Jesus, will find its initial fulfilment as the extraordinary figures "from the East" stride on to the stage in Chapter 2.

The Names of Jesus:

Matthew's first chapter, densely packed with persuasive insights into who Jesus is for new and would-be believers of the 1st and 21st centuries, concludes with the briefest account of the birth of Jesus, in Bethlehem, and his two significant names. Openness to God in dreams is crucial in this and the next chapter as God's purposes are worked out through the Holy Family and the travelling astrologers who come in search of them.

In a dream, Joseph is assured that he should not fear to take Mary as his wife – what courage he displays to hitch his reputation, his future to the assurance of a dream, and to name his adopted son:

Jesus.

Jesus was a common enough name in the Palestine of the 1st century. It was essentially the same as the name "Joshua", the hero from ancient times who had brought the Israelites into the Promised Land. But in his dream, Joseph is reminded of its oft-forgotten meaning, "for he shall save his people from their sins." Jesus the Saviour. How profoundly true and accurate this name will be, in ways far beyond Joseph's comprehension now. It will shape Jesus' whole life. It will take him to the cross, where his name and its meaning will be flung back in his teeth:

> In the same way the chief priests, the teachers of the law and the elders mocked him, "He saved others," they said, "but he can't save himself!" (Matt 27:41-2)

Immanuel.

At this point Matthew inserts the first of five scripture passages that will underline the fulfilment of prophecy that is taking place in Jesus:

> All this took place to fulfil what the Lord said through the prophet: "The virgin will be with child and will give birth to a son, and they will call him Immanuel" – which means, "God with us." (1:23)

God with us! Immanuel! As far as we know it was not ever used as an alternative name socially or publicly for Jesus but it has been beloved of Christians through the ages, capturing the heart of the incarnation, and capturing what has been at the heart of

Christian experience continually. In Jesus, God has come to be with us, and continues to be with us through life's journey.

And it appears to be a profoundly important truth for Matthew himself. The final words of his Gospel and the final words of Jesus before the ascension are, "And surely I am with you always, to the very end of the age." (28:20)

"Immanuel" in China

In November 2013 I travelled for the first time to China at the invitation of the Bible Society. Most of our 10 days were spent in Nanjing and the towns and cities within about a 100-mile radius. We visited a number of churches during that time, all belonging to the state-recognised Three-Self Patriotic Movement / China Christian Council network of churches. Some were large urban churches, full of students and young professionals, others rural and smaller. In all these churches I noticed that on the front wall was the same display – a large central cross, often bright red, and four Chinese characters, usually two on each side of the cross. I asked what the meaning was and why it was so commonly displayed. During the Cultural Revolution, I was told, when all the churches were closed, pastors imprisoned or even killed, and Christians persecuted, the name "Immanuel" was used as a secret sign between Christians – rather like the fish sign in early Christian history - as a word of encouragement, and a way of identifying a Christian brother or sister: "Immanuel – God is with us!" – even in the midst of these horrors." It was also the truth that we experienced during those years.

These four characters are the four syllables of the word Immanuel."

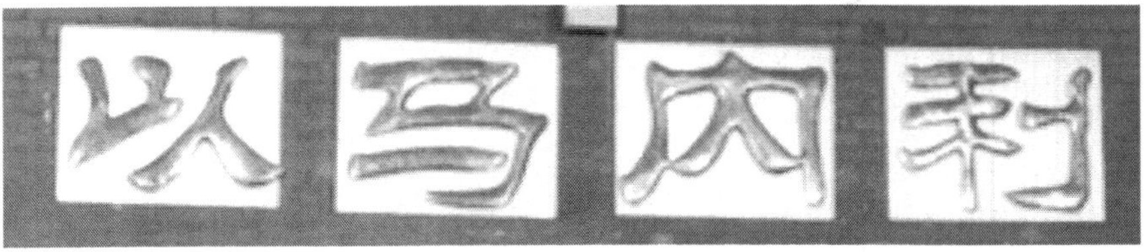

The church in the Nanjing area – the scene of the horrific Nanjing Massacre during the Second World War as well as a focus of the Cultural Revolution – still holds on passionately to that history and that truth.

It has been a theme that Matthew was concerned to highlight during the course of his Gospel – the repeated commitment of Jesus to "be with" his disciples. "For where two or three come together in my name, there am I with them." (18:20)

Maybe it is time now to meet the Magi!

Three Magi in leopard-print leggings....; © Holly Hayes;
Detail of nave mosaic in Sant'Apollinare Nuovo, Ravenna;
http://www.sacred-destinations.com/italy/ravenna-st-apollinare-nuovo

CHAPTER 3

MAGI, STAR & CALL

Matthew Chapter 2:

> **1** After Jesus was born in Bethlehem in Judea, during the time of King Herod, Magi from the east came to Jerusalem **2** and asked, "Where is the one who has been born king of the Jews? We saw his star when it rose and have come to worship him."

MAGI

Who were the Magi?

The Magi have made a long, colourful and exotic journey into the western imagination. Kings, Wise Men, three in number, with royal and privileged bearing, crowns, fabulous gifts. . . . From early in Christian history there were paintings and mosaics representing these visitors to the Christ Child. The famous and very beautiful mosaic in the Basilica of Sant' Apollinaire Nuovo in Ravenna, made in the 6th century, has already settled on the number of three, and has given them the names that are still familiar to us, Balthazar, Melchior and Gaspar.

Farcical Journey

Persians not Arabs,
Farsi not Arabic,
Magi not Kings,
Worship not rule.

Crazy and farcical,
Leaving two rivers,
To follow a star,
To worship a King,
A journey afar.

Leaving behind
Family and kin,
Like Abram of old,
Unlike the King,
Outside his line.

In the mosaic these three represent the different Ages of Man – a young man, a middle aged and an elderly man – all ages are welcome to bring their gifts. But the multi-cultural interpretation that later became common is not yet evident. During the Middle Ages it became common for one of the Magi or at least one of the retainers to be shown as an African, and others from different Asian or even Chinese backgrounds. In the Ravenna mosaic, as in the Bethlehem mosaic of the same period but now lost, these men are most definitely Persian and are shown in distinctive Persian dress, with Parthian caps.

But kings they were not. It is not at all surprising that early in Christian history they were represented and described as "kings". Christian minds went quickly to Psalm 72, which seemed to describe the Magi visit wonderfully well. The psalm, notionally speaking of Solomon, was always considered to be messianic, speaking of how through a king in David's line, the Abrahamic promise would come to fulfilment as kings bowed down before him:

> He will rule from sea to sea, and from the River to the ends of the earth.
> The desert tribes will bow before him and his enemies will lick the dust.
> The kings of Tarshish and of distant shores will bring tribute to him;
> The kings of Sheba and Seba will bring him gifts.
> All kings will bow down before him and all nations serve him. (Psalm 72:8-11)

A verse from Isaiah also appeared prophetic of the Magi story:

> Nations will come to your light
> And kings to the brightness of your dawn. (Isaiah 60:3)

Theologically Isaiah and the psalmist were right on target – the visit of the Magi did indeed signify the coming of the nations to worship the new King, the beginning of a global fulfilment of the promise to Abraham.

The description of the mysterious visitors as "Kings" became particularly dominant after Emperor Constantine in the early 4th century, when emperors and kings wanted to portray themselves as faithful Christians, who have bowed before Christ, and who can claim the loyalty of all Christian people.

Their description as "Wise Men" is more modern, developing mostly after the Renaissance and particularly during the Enlightenment – when the potential of human wisdom and reason was being affirmed both in Church and society. Whether as Kings or Wise Men, the Magi made better sense – God was calling the best of pagan society, its royalty and its philosophers, to lay their wealth, in its various forms at the feet of Jesus. The best in society was affirmed, church and society would bless and encourage each other. In fact, Matthew's message, and the message his hearers heard, was far more disturbing. These first visitors were not royal, were not "wise" in conventional terms – in fact God was calling those with absolutely nothing to commend them. Their skills, their wisdom counted for nothing here – here it was just ignorance and superstition. Yet they are the ones God called. Such is Grace, such is the abundant, indiscriminate love of God.

In the Book of Daniel, Magi play an important role – the emptiness and folly of their ways is contrasted with Daniel's resourcing by the God of heaven. When King Nebuchadnezzar king of Babylon urgently needs a dream interpreted – surely the natural territory of the Magi - they are unable to help. So the king turns to Daniel. "Are you able to tell what I saw in my dream and interpret it?"

> Daniel replied, "No wise man, enchanter, magician or diviner can explain to the king the mystery he has asked about. But there is a God in heaven who reveals mysteries." (Daniel 2:27-28)

That is the framework in which we need to understand the Magi. It is the "God in heaven" who is directing operations here, bringing pagan astrologers to the feet of Christ.

In Western telling of the story, they were sometimes Magi, sometimes Kings, sometimes Wise Men. But in the 1st century, the Magi carried with them the odour of occultism and superstition. That is a major part of the troubling character of Matthew's story. Even in 2000, during the Millennium Peace Pilgrimage, which re-enacted the journey, as the pilgrims found their way through Iraq and Jordan, they found it wiser to speak of "Wise Men", rather than "Magi". The word still had its dark edge. They were easier and safer companions as Wise Men. Elderly, gentle and sage.

Indeed the word "magi", "magoi" in Greek, is the source of our English words "magic" and "magician." Clearly also in New Testament times the word had become virtually synonymous with occultism, sorcery and magic.

Simon Magus the sorcerer or magician whose story is told in Acts 8:9ff is one such example as is Elymas the magus sorcerer in Acts 13:8.

Do we perhaps need to rewrite our nativity play scripts?

The Magi and the Zoroastrians

So who were the Magi? It is easier to say who they were not than who they were! Very few documents on any subject survive from the Parthian period in Persia (247 BC – AD 224). Herodotus, the Greek historian of the 5th century BC, wrote at some length about Magi, describing them as one of the tribes of the Medes from the southern steppes of Central Asia who migrated into the Persian Empire around the 6th century BC and who served there as priests and diviners under successive dynasties. It appears that over subsequent centuries they were sometimes in and sometimes out of favour with Persia's rulers, sometimes needed for their divining and cultic skills and their counsel, but never fully trusted. Often close to the throne, but vulnerable and dispensable.

As a result, over time, they could be found in many of the lands that the Persian Empire had conquered at some point. We hear of Magi as priests and political advisors in Persia (Iran), in Mesopotamia (Iraq and Syria) in Asia Minor (Turkey) and in Armenia. It is possible too that there were influential Magi in Alexandria as by the 1st century it was a renowned centre for a number of the phenomena with which the Magi were often associated – astrology, astronomy, eastern-style occultism and the cult of Mithras (which had reached the Mediterranean from Persia).

In 66 AD, illustrating their widespread influence, King Tiridates of Armenia came, together with three princes from neighbouring kingdoms, to pay homage to Nero in Rome, describing himself and his companions as of Parthian descent. Pliny, interestingly, describes Tiridates and his companions as "magi".

So whilst the Magi who came to Jerusalem and Bethlehem in the last years of Herod the Great would have been regarded as strange and unusual visitors, perhaps evoking a measure of fear and mistrust, they were not without history or context.

Consistently they were associated with astrology, with sorcery and with occult religious practice, and sometimes also with Zoroastrianism. The evidence for this is by no means straightforward. In some contexts – particularly in Persia itself where the religion was strongest – the magi may even have become Zoroastrian priests. In other contexts they are described as hostile to the Persian religion. Maybe both are true, depending on the location.

The origins and the nature of Zoroastrianism itself are likewise far from clear. It is very uncertain when the founder Zoroaster lived (possibly sometime in the period 1400-1000BC). It is uncertain what he taught – certainly Zoroastrianism meant very different things at different times. At times it proclaimed many gods, and borrowed extensively from the Greeks, at other times it taught a dualism between the forces of good and evil where human beings were urged to align themselves with the good. It was commonly associated, and still is, with fire altars and fire worship. Were our Magi Zoroastrian priests? It is very unlikely – but in the first century Zoroastrianism was gaining strength in the Persian Empire, and after 224AD became the state religion and forcefully persecuted other religions. After the Islamic conquest in 651 AD, Zoroastrians became a small minority in Persia. Today the few thousand that remain can be found mainly in India where they fled for refuge after the Islamic conquest of Iran, and where they are known as Parsis.

Where were these Magi from?

By the time of the birth of Jesus, groups of Magi could be found all over the eastern Mediterranean. Some early Christian writers, such as Justin Martyr, considered that the Bethlehem Magi came from Arabia on the grounds that their gifts distinctively come from that area. Frankincense, in particular, can only be found in Arabia and Somalia. But these were expensive commodities widely traded through the Middle East. Our choice has to be somewhere in Mesopotamia and beyond, in the territories of the Parthian Empire that covered modern day Iran and Iraq. Early Christian art commonly represented them in characteristic Persian dress. Ctesiphon was the western capital of the Parthian Empire where Magi would certainly have been a significant presence. Ctesiphon was about 20 miles south of modern day Baghdad on the banks of the Tigris River. It became a significant centre after the expulsion of the Greeks when the new Parthian dynasty made it their winter home. By the time of the birth of Jesus Ctesiphon had become a major urban centre. By the 6th century it was possibly the largest city in the world, before Byzantine and then Arab attacks led to its decline. Today all that can be seen is a large and magnificent ruined gateway.

Babylon (30 odd miles further south on the banks of the Euphrates) had, by the first century, ceased to exist.

However, in the wider region there were still significant communities of Jews who had not returned from the exile in the 6th century BC.

Ctesiphon would have been a major centre for Persian Magi. It was a major urban centre where their astrological, occult and divining gifts would have found a ready market and close to the court for every possibility of gaining royal favour or the royal ear. They were not kings or royalty. At their most prominent they may have been advisors to kings. At other times they may have been very marginal in Parthian society, as they often evoked fear and mistrust. With Jewish communities still around, they might nonetheless have been well aware of Jewish expectations of a Messiah or King for the Jews.

Matthew, however, simply says that they are "from the East" (2:1). Whilst they were almost certainly from Ctesiphon or the Babylonia region more broadly, the very openness of this phrase has encouraged Christians of many countries to the east to find themselves in the story, and to develop traditions of their own about astrologers and wise men seeking the Christ Child. Such stories have developed in India and China, and elsewhere, in art and drama and literature. And commonly the Magi approach the Christ Child in the dress and custom of these countries. Whilst clearly an elaboration of Matthew's narrative, these stories are in line with Matthew's intention to signal that in Christ the gracious invitation of God, always present in Israel's history, goes out to all nations. It reaches beyond all the boundaries of ethnicity, religion and culture, which seem so far to have excluded them, to welcome them in.

History is not that helpful in elucidating just who the Magi were. But it tells us enough to help us grasp why they were so significant to Matthew. In chapter 1 he has laid a compelling foundation as he seeks to ground new Jewish and Gentile disciples of Jesus in their new Faith. Through the genealogy he has laid out the grounds for accepting Jesus as both Son of David and Son of Abraham, heir to God's promises through them. In a simple description of his birth, the emphasis is on Jesus as the Son of David. He is the one who saves his people from their sins. He is Immanuel – the one who is God with us.

Now comes his first big narrative, in which the emphasis will shift to Jesus as the one who fulfils the promises to Abraham, that through his offspring all nations on earth will be blessed (Gen. 22: 18). This story will seek to tease out the meaning of the coming amongst us of the God-with-Us Saviour. What is this like? How will we recognise his coming? Matthew has already alerted us to the possibility that there may be surprises, that this may not be the story we expect. The four mothers in the Messiah's lineage, with their foreign origins and their irregular personal stories, have already alerted us to the fact that the God who is now making himself known in Jesus is unpredictable, he changes the rules as he goes. He works by grace and surprise. In the turmoil of human life and struggle he retains his providential freedom. His promises will be fulfilled and his love for all the peoples of the earth, heralded in the covenantal promises to Abraham and to David, will triumph.

We are ready for a surprise – but perhaps not *this* surprise. We don't know if Matthew had other birth stories of Jesus available to him, or whether this was all he had in the research folder. But this one, if we hear it right, provides us with a shocking and mind-changing encounter.

Who are the first people who come striding, or riding on their camels, into our view? Who are the first people stirred up by God to come to meet his Son? To bow before him in homage and worship? Well, it is yet more foreigners, more strangers from afar. These are astrologers, sorcerers, pagan priests, diviners, outsiders. They were certainly not men worthy of respect in Jewish circles, not Kings, and not Wise Men either. They are the embodiment of pagan ignorance and folly.

These were men who were way outside all the recognised boundaries of God's people. They were wholly untaught in the Torah, and completely unaware of Israel's prophetic expectation – unless they had picked something up back in Mesopotamia from the Jewish communities there. They were without the moral and ritual framework that kept God's people on the straight and narrow. These are the first to beat their way to Mary and Joseph's door in Bethlehem. And very probably, they don't even really quite know why they were here, and what they were witnessing. They were exactly the kind of people whose divinations and speculations Isaiah so despised:

> Keep on, then, with your magic spells and with your many sorceries,
> which you have laboured at since childhood. . . .
> Let your astrologers come forward,
> those stargazers who make predictions month by month,
> let them save you from what is coming upon you.
> Surely they are like stubble; the fire will burn them up. (Isaiah 47:12-14)

But now indeed, the first are last, and the last have become first. How did this go down in Matthew's local Jewish / Christian assembly? Did Romans and Greek-speakers rejoice in it? Could Jewish believers in Jesus see that it was at last the radical fulfilling of all that Israel had longed for over the centuries? Or was it all a bit unsettling? Would something a bit more moderate, a bit more middle of the road have been more acceptable? Or did they just romanticise the story, as we do?

If we open it up a little more, what is Matthew trying to tease out here? Let us imagine for a moment, that, as some scholars have supposed, Matthew's home church was in Antioch (the third city of the Roman Empire, after Rome and Alexandria). It is for this congregation that he is primarily writing, maybe as early as AD 65, maybe later around 80 AD, as most scholars would argue. Around AD 35 this church had been the centre of a remarkable and imaginative experiment (Acts 11:19ff). Following the martyrdom of Stephen, some of the Jerusalem Christians fled northwards to Antioch. They were converts from Judaism; some of them local Palestinian Aramaic- speakers, and some of them probably from other parts of the Mediterranean and Greek-speaking. In Antioch, unfazed by the events in Jerusalem, they continued to share the Gospel with those they met. Some of them decided that the logic of the Gospel was that the good news of Jesus was for everyone, and they began for the first time to share the Gospel with Greek-speakers with no Jewish background. These people were Greek in language and culture, with no Jewish grounding. And, Acts tells us, "a great number believed and turned to the Lord." This was the founding story of the Antioch Church, and it became the base for Paul's missionary explorations into Turkey and beyond. Here, Matthew is calling them back to that heritage – the heritage of a courageous and risky sharing of the Gospel across cultural and religious boundaries. He is calling them back to the heritage of being, despite many difficulties, a new kind of Christian community of different cultures, honouring each other, and worshipping, eating and witnessing together.

The Magi story has some similarities to the famous story of Peter and Cornelius in Acts 10-11, where the inner turmoil that Peter went through in order to be ready to share the Gospel with a Roman centurion is graphically told. In this story Matthew is saying clearly to his readers: this is what the Gospel means! It means crossing cultures, receiving those we have previously despised or excluded.

It means patiently building new kinds of community that we previously would have rejected. In fact God has taken the initiative to call such people first as a sign of the shape of the new people he is making. Straightaway, in Matthew's second chapter, we are face to face with the radical challenge of the Gospel to embrace all the change and transformation involved in God's promise to bless all the nations of the world through his Son, and through his people.

It is the Gospel itself that we need to hear afresh:

> Brothers, think of what you were when you were called. Not many of you were wise by human standards; not many were influential, not many were of noble birth. But God chose the foolish things of the world to shame the wise; God chose the weak things if the world to shame the strong. He chose the lowly things and the despised things. . . (I Cor 1: 26-28)

The Hinge Turns

The innovative disciples in Antioch, Peter and Cornelius in Caesarea, the Ethiopian eunuch whom the evangelist Philip met, the Magi in faraway Mesopotamia: all represent the new age dawning with the coming of Christ, the turning of a door hinge that opens a new way. Distinguished Scottish historian and missiologist Andrew Walls some years ago called this moment the "Ephesian Moment"[i]. He based his explanation particularly on the second chapter of Ephesians where the cross of Christ is described as having broken down the walls of hostility between Jews and Gentiles and as having made possible a new kind of community – a new humanity - where people of different cultures and languages discovered in their life together what being a disciple of Jesus meant in their own culture. This new community, united in devotion to Christ, sharing worship, fellowship and eating together, nonetheless explored faithfulness to Christ within their own culture and context – finding as it were a new, a third culture. This new community, unified in worship of Jesus, but diverse in background was a demonstration to the world of the new humanity that God in Christ was bringing into being.

Andrew Walls' startling suggestion is that we are again, following centuries of various forms of cultural imperialism in the Church and in our evangelism, entering an "Ephesian Moment" in the World Church. In this "Moment" there is again the freedom of Christians across the world to explore both our unity in Christ, and the diversity in discipleship that we are each called to in the specifics of our lives and contexts. With it we will experience conflict and misunderstanding as we struggle to learn and live together.

So, the extraordinary growth of the World Church in our day is no longer driven by the great traditions and denominations of the West and its mission agencies, from centres in Rome, Canterbury or elsewhere, by European theological expertise, or even by the money of the West – but by the Pentecostalism of the Brazilian Church, the evangelistic passion of the Nigerian Church, the organisation and thoroughness of the Korean Church and the extraordinary energy of the burgeoning Chinese Church, and many others beside. And those of us in the West may often find them uncomfortable companions, as were the Greeks and Romans pushing their way into the Antioch Church, or, indeed, the Magi making their way to Bethlehem.

STAR

The Magi and their Star

Christmas has two great symbols – the Angel who greeted the shepherds and the Star that led the Magi. And this star is quite simply the most famous star in history. Immense numbers of books and articles have been written to try and unravel its mysteries. What was it exactly, and how did it "lead" the Magi?

One thing is plain. The Magi, wherever they were found, were known to be expert in the study and interpretation of the stars, and Matthew's account affirms that. They lived in an age of increasing speculation about the stars and their influence on human affairs. This was the period in which the Zodiac was developed as a way of mapping and interrelating the planets and the constellations, thus making horoscopes based on people's birth date possible. The Jews fiercely rejected all such mechanisms that by-passed the providence of God.

So, what kind of phenomenon was the Star? There have basically been four main proposals, each passionately championed in its time.

a) A nova or supernova. A nova is a short-lived bright light in the sky when a dying star eventually implodes in a great burst of light. It might last a few weeks or months. The 17th c astronomer Johannes Kepler strongly promoted this possibility. Detailed research has not produced any report of such an event close to the birth of Jesus.

b) A comet. Comets have caught human imagination throughout history. The most famous of comets, Halley's Comet, made an appearance in 12-11 BC, too early to be associated with the birth of Jesus. In any case, generally in human history, comets have been associated with catastrophes rather than celebrations.

c) A Conjunction of Planets. If the explanation is a naturally occurring phenomenon, the most satisfactory explanation is undoubtedly a conjunction of significant planets, creating a brighter light. We now know that there were conjunctions of Jupiter and Saturn in May/June, in September/ October and in December of 7BC. This is a very rare event and would allow for the appearance of the star when the Magi were still in Persia or Mesopotamia, and again to guide them from Jerusalem to Bethlehem. We are less than certain about the significance given to such events in the first century and before, but Jupiter could be associated with a major world ruler and Saturn was associated with the people of the western lands, and could include the Jews. The appearance of such a star in the constellation of Pisces could have indicated an event associated with the last days. Rather speculatively, it has been suggested that such a conjunction could have been interpreted at the time of Jesus to mean that there would appear a new king amongst the Jews, a world ruler for the last days. Whilst this explanation probably is the most persuasive, it is still quite speculative.

d) A Divine Provision. This might all seem highly speculative, and much of it relies on matters of which we are very uncertain or ignorant. A natural explanation of course does not mean that the Magi's star is devoid of divine meaning. But the inconclusive nature of these explanations has persuaded many people to think of it as a miraculous provision without a natural origin.

Matthew's Readers

Many of the elements in Matthew's story that we may find puzzling or difficult to accept would not have troubled his original readers in the same way. Unusual sights in the heavens were commonly associated with public events. In an extraordinary coincidence, when Julius Caesar died in 44 BC, a nova appeared in the sky over his funeral pyre. This was understood to be a new star, and persuaded everyone that Caesar had indeed gone to join the gods! [ii] Even though Jews at this time sternly rejected these connections, they were well aware of their prevalence in the world around. But by the 5th century, for example, it was possible even for a synagogue such as the one at Sepphoris, a few miles from Nazareth, to have a Zodiac diagram mosaic on the floor.[iii]

It was also well-known for foreign dignitaries to travel long distances to congratulate or offer homage to other rulers. When Herod completed the building of Caesarea Maritima on the Mediterranean coast in 10-9 BC, ambassadors and dignitaries came from many countries bringing lavish gifts[iv].

But also, this story, as do so many of the stories in the Gospels, reminded people of Old Testament prophesies that seemed compellingly fulfilled in the coming of Jesus. Matthew uses five Old Testament passages in the section from 1:18 to 2:23 to illustrate how these events fulfil prophetic expectation[v]. The rather startling parallel to this passage that Matthew clearly has in mind as he writes is the story of Balaam (and his amazing talking donkey) in Numbers 22-24. Note the parallels between the Magi and this Old Testament seer:

- Balaam is a seer, a diviner, from Mesopotamia, "near the River". He is, as it were, a magus. (Nu 22:5)
- When called by Balak to bring a curse upon the Israelites who were passing through Moab and Midian, he is physically and psychologically unable to do so, but can only bring blessings, as the Magi also did. (Nu 23:6-10 & 24:19). His prophecy looks forward to the coming of Christ, and would have been so understood by Matthew:

> The oracle of Balaam, son of Peor,
> the oracle of one who sees clearly,
> the oracle of one who hears the words of God. . . .
>
> A star will come out of Jacob;
> A sceptre will rise out of Israel.
> He will crush the foreheads of Moab, . .
> A Ruler will come out of Jacob. . . (Nu 24: 15-19)

Balaam is one of a number of Old Testament figures, "pagans" who blessed Israel, reversing the Abrahamic promise that Israel would bless the nations. Others were: Melchizedek, king of Salem who blessed Abraham himself (Gen 14:18); Jethro, Moses' Midianite father in law and advisor, and a priest amongst his own people, (Ex 3:1), and Rahab the Jericho prostitute whom we have already met. It is as if, from time to time, God needs to educate his people from the outside, teaching them how to be a blessing to the nations. We might reflect on more modern figures, such as Gandhi or Nelson Mandela, outside the Christian community, who have fulfilled such a role, demonstrating how God blesses people when the Church seems to have forgotten how.

1400 years after Balaam, other magi, - astrologers and pagan priests - played a similar role, being the first to bring worship and offerings to the feet of the King of Kings. Perhaps on the banks of the Euphrates or the Tigris, they saw a new star, rising above the eastern horizon. Using all the interpretative skills at their disposal, immersed in their own worldview, reflecting on what they hear of hopes and expectations amongst the Jewish community in the city, perhaps considering the delicate political issues of the region, they agree together that it speaks of a King newly born amongst the Jews, whose significance is universal. They decide to leave home and family, knowing they will be away for some months, perhaps years, leave their religious and political duties, gather precious gifts fit for a king, assemble their finances, their supplies, their servants, horses and camels . . . and go!

Bruner in his commentary, quoting others, sums this up compellingly:

> The *theological* meaning of Matthew's star is that '*every* expectation is fulfilled in Jesus, not only that of the Old Testament, but also the expectation of the whole natural world as well: here is the world-king whom *all* await'. [vi]

As Bruner goes on to say, this, truly, is "Jesu, Joy of Man's Desiring." The very one who, in Isaiah's words, has no beauty that we should desire him, is actually the one who fulfils all the desire and longing of the nations, all that human aspiration ultimately is reaching after. And the star will lead these earliest representatives of that desire to the modest home in Bethlehem where the fulfilment lies.

> Sages, leave your contemplations;
> Brighter visions beam afar;
> Seek the great Desire of Nations;
> Ye have seen his natal star!
> (Charles Wesley, 'Angels from the Realms of Glory')

> I will shake all nations, and the desired of all nations will come.
> (Haggai 2:6)

CALL

The Call of the Magi

Like all the best stories, Matthew's story of the Magi operates at several levels. It is, in the first place, however its essentials came into his possession, a dramatic narrative taking forward the story of the infant Jesus, from his birth in Bethlehem, fulfilling ancient prophecy, to the settling of the family in the obscure Galilean town of Nazareth. "Can anything good come out of Nazareth?", as the future disciple Nathaniel asked (Jn 1:46). This story enables Matthew to demonstrate his overarching claim, that Jesus of Nazareth, crucified under Pontius Pilate, is Israel's long-awaited Messiah, son of Abraham, son of David, heir to all the promises to Israel.

But the story also serves other functions for Matthew. It reveals what that new beginning really looks like, how it will work out in the world, how it will impact the nations of the world. It is, in a way, a distillation, a parable of what the Gospel will mean as, in obedience to Jesus' final words at the close of the Gospel, his disciples "go and make disciples of all nations" (Matt 28:19)

What the Magi do not know is that the God of Israel, the one true God, the Creator God, is now taking decisive action to fulfil his promises and the dreams of Israel as, far away, a unique baby boy comes into the world. They are following their instincts, their speculations, the traditions of their profession – but it is this God, as yet unknown to them, who is stirring them up and moving them out on a journey that will be the journey of their lives.

Right at this point in the story, there is a sharp lesson for all those of us accustomed to living within established Christian communities. God's heart is for all peoples, and the disciples of Jesus need always to be willing to reach beyond the frontiers they are accustomed to – for he is already there, already stirring people up to seek for him. They are stirred up, or events they cannot control move them on and out, they are called, within their own world, the only world they can understand. They may not know who or what is stirring them up, they may not know where the journey will lead them, they cannot imagine the outcome. They may be refugees rather than travellers. But the

God who calls his people to bless the nations, the God who in Jesus is the God-with-us Saviour, the God who stirred up the Magi in distant Ctesiphon, is on their case. God's people need to have eyes and ears, need to have imagination, for what he is up to and for whom they may need to welcome from across strange boundaries of politics, culture, language and worldview. It is always a surprise.

What we can now begin to see is that this is an ever-widening, community-building, Christ-acknowledging, reconciling and healing movement, drawing people in with all their diversities, spreading across the whole world.

Called from Beyond the Margins

The Magi are the pioneering examples of the unpredictable way of building God's kingdom that would in time unfold : God taking the initiative and finding people where they are, revealing Christ to them within their own culture, and making of them contextual disciples.

> In short the narrative does not portray the Magi as wise men whose learning leads them to Christ, but as ignorant people to whom God reveals the Christ.
> (Powell , 2001, p. 155)

We have seen it ourselves, we may have experienced it ourselves. What might it look like in a diversity of contexts?

A hero of mine, early in my African experience, was Apolo Kivebulaya. Kivebulaya had been a soldier with a particularly brutal history during the political and religious wars that plagued Uganda at the close of the 19th century. He met Christ and became a Christian through the witness of the early generation of CMS (Church Missionary Society) missionaries. The rest of his life was devoted to taking the healing and peace-making Gospel he had encountered to far areas of Uganda and Congo. He was a true cross-cultural missionary, deeply committed to the reality of God's love for all peoples. His first years were spent amongst the Toro people of western Uganda. From there he felt God calling him beyond the Ruwenzori Mountains to the peoples there. Towards the end of his life he began to carry the Gospel to the pygmy people of the Congo jungles. Before he died (in 1933), he asked to be buried with his feet towards the jungle where the pygmy people lived[vii].

During the long, brutal civil war in South Sudan (1983-2005), Reuben Macir was one of the few experienced and senior clergy who stayed with his people throughout. During that time he was made a bishop. It was a time of dramatic church growth as many thousands of the Dinka people in the villages and cattle camps turned to Christ. To support this growth he started a Bible Training School at Dhiaukuei, a remote settlement, deep in the pastoral grasslands of the Dinka country. They received no resources from outside. All the buildings were of local grass and wattle construction. There were no books, other than the handful that people already possessed, and such New Testaments and Prayer Books as had survived the war. Dhiaukuei was a dynamic centre of Christian life, learning, worship and witness.

Part of the college programme was to take all the students out on evangelism in the villages. "What did you do? What was your message?" I asked. Reuben replied that nearly always they found that God had already been at work, the people were ready to receive them. They were already reading what parts of the Bible they had. Often a local person had already started gathering people together for prayers. Often the people were already experiencing healing in response to prayer to Jesus (in the war, all regular medical services had collapsed). Barren women, and cattle for that matter, were bearing offspring. What was needed was some teaching, baptism of the people, and the appointment of a local leader as the leader of prayers. . . . and to arrange to come again to follow up. And in some villages, at the request of the people, and even the traditional priest, local spirit shrines would be destroyed. It sounded very much like New Testament and Early Church times!

Aziz (not his real name) grew up in Iran during the Islamic Revolution in a family known for rather secular and radical political views. Life was always insecure. Eventually his brother fled the country for fear of arrest, and several years later, Aziz followed. He travelled across Turkey and across Europe, as many did, locked in the back of a truck. Eventually he found his way to Britain and applied for political asylum. He was confident he would be accepted as his brother had already been accepted and had a good job. Five years later he was no further forward, awaiting an appeal, unemployed, time on his hands, no future, rather depressed. Contact with Iranian Christians in Britain he had found unwelcoming and intimidating. One day, depressed and lonely, he walked into St Saviour's Church and began to find some friends. In time he and I began to meet for an hour or more every Friday afternoon. Our first purpose was to read Luke's Gospel together, but very soon we found that in addition we needed to attend to, and try to interpret, a stream of provocative dreams he was receiving. Was God speaking in these dreams? For two years we debated both dreams and the gospel, weaving together his experience of Islam, his encounter with the Christian scriptures, his experience on the streets of Surrey, and his dreams. Sometimes he thought he believed, mostly he sat on the fence. One day he said to me, "I think I am a Christian!" It turned out that in a dramatic dream, he was caught up in a Middle Eastern street battle. He took refuge in a church, or rather, he was rescued and pulled inside by Christian priests. He knew instinctively that this was where he belonged. Sculptures of Christ reassured him. Christians welcomed him. He felt he had at last made a commitment and had, in a sense, come home.

Later we baptized Aziz. Quietly, on a Wednesday night, with only his Alpha Group present (themselves at all stages of Christian commitment) and a few friends. He told his story of meeting Christ – travelling thousands of miles, wrestling with scripture and his dreams, finding a home in a strange English church community.

The Journey of the Magi; James Tissot; Brooklyn Museum, NY

CHAPTER 4.

PILGRIMAGE

Matthew Chapter 2:

> **2** "Where is the one who has been born king of the Jews? We saw his star when it rose and have come to worship him."

The Cost of Pilgrimage

When God calls, whether to our first discovery of Christ, or to some new task of discipleship, or a changed way of life, it always involves journey. That is the nature of life. Every day, inevitably, we journey on in life. The question is whether we are also pilgrims, hearing God's call, seeking him as our true home and destiny. All Christian pilgrimage is in the end, a call to Jesus.

Pilgrimage has from early times been a part of Christian spirituality. Helena, mother of Emperor Constantine, visited the Holy Land in the early 4th century, seeking to identify the

Through Centuries

From the beginning,
Magi pondered and travelled;
offered and worshipped.

For the record,
Matthew collected taxes and stories;
scribed and described.

In the sermon,
Lancelot Andrews
translated and prayed;
preached for the King.

Through the poem,
T S Eliot essayed and imagined;
journeyed to Christ.

major sites of the ministry, crucifixion and resurrection of Christ. The outcome was a very durable mixture of the highly likely and the highly uncertain. The desire to see the places where the central events of Jesus' life occurred has been a powerful element in Christian devotion from then until the present day. In the Church of the Holy Sepulchre in Jerusalem, I was moved last summer to see rows and rows of meticulously carved crosses, each about two inches high, from the era of the Crusades, each representing the eventual arrival at the site of Christ's crucifixion and resurrection of a weary pilgrim. Such pilgrimage, with its difficulties, cost, risk and danger (now mainly lost through air travel) is a powerful picture of the Christian life, and engaging in pilgrimage is a powerful way of deepening that life.

Pilgrimage is no longer just a Christian or religious enterprise. The historic pilgrim ways in Europe – to Canterbury, to Santiago, to Trondheim, or to the Holy Land – attract many people looking for something deeper, a meaning for life, a shaping experience, the community of travelling with others on a similar search. The Danish Lutheran Church for some years has supported a pastor to accompany pilgrims and help them profit from their journeying, to develop the awareness and the skills of reflection that will enable the pilgrimage to have a life-changing impact. Whilst much modern pilgrimage is not intentionally Christian, it is for the pilgrim a time of openness in which new things can happen and in which the God who acts in surprising ways in and through surprising people can move.

Matthew tells his story incisively, with brevity, passing over the weeks and months that the Magi had travelled from Ctesiphon or elsewhere.

"We have seen his star in the east, and we have come. . ."

We cannot know what they experienced on the way. But we should understand them in a way as the first Christian pilgrims, not fully knowing what they are about, but setting out on a demanding search for Christ, not knowing what the impact and outcome of that encounter will be.

Poets and other writers however have pondered that hidden phase of the story. And artists have commonly portrayed the long journey. T S Eliot's famous poem mainly concerns the hardships, regrets and cost of the journey:

> A cold coming we had of it,
> Just the worst time of the year
> For a journey. . .
>
> A hard time we had of it.
>
> With the voices singing in our ears, saying
> That this was all folly

And the regret and missing of home:

> There were times we regretted
> The summer palaces on slopes, the terraces,
> And the silken girls bringing sherbet.

But there is no other way to obey the call, follow the star, to come to the feet of the King. Pilgrimage demands perseverance, endurance and faith.

The Reward of Pilgrimage

At the time that I was beginning this book, I was overnighting at the Bield, a retreat centre near Perth in Scotland. I was on my way, on pilgrimage, to Iona, and from there to a tiny wooden cabin in Sutherland in search of rest and solitude, a new direction for my ministry and, I trusted, some new encounter with God. In the morning, at the community prayers, Melitta, one of the staff members at the Bield, read from the story of Elijah at Mount Horeb (I Kings 19), and underlined the Lord's challenging question to Elijah,

> "What are you doing here, Elijah?"

(In fact the probing question is asked twice!) It was a question for pilgrimage. Elijah himself had arrived at Horeb after a desperate flight from Jezebel who had sworn to kill him. Hungry and exhausted, he fled to the Source, to the place where it all began, where Israel's journey with her covenant God had commenced, hardly knowing what he wanted.

I was pinned to the bench in the little chapel, knowing immediately it was the question that would stay with me through the following month. Why are you here – do you even know? What are you looking for? Are they the right things? Are you just escaping? Are you here for the truly important things? Are you ready for a new beginning, new challenges? How will you be when you go home? I knew I had come for rest, for quiet, for recovery after several demanding and draining years. And beyond that I knew I wanted, I needed, a renewing and refreshing touch from God. I wanted to get to "Horeb" and to

hear that gentle whisper, that still, small voice. Maybe, at the Bield, I was already hearing it.
For the following four weeks I travelled with Elijah as my companion, to Iona and in Sutherland. The weather was wonderful, the countryside wild and exhilarating, but the emotional journey was turbulent. I journeyed with Elijah. I recollected with him, as it were, the exhilaration of battles won, where the Spirit and adrenalin had flowed. I too knew something of what it is to run before the Lord in the power of the Spirit and in a rush of adrenalin. I recalled the pain and confusion of difficult times and of rejection. I resonated with Elijah's exhaustion and his need for sleep. Indeed I slept very deeply. I said the Daily Office. I kept long periods of silence and as much solitude as I could, bearing in mind the occasional need for a visit to the Spar grocery. I left my CDs behind – knowing that music had always been one of the ways that I shut out the unsettling possibilities of quiet. At times, from somewhere deep in my soul, I felt sad, or anxious. And I even climbed a mountain with Elijah as my imaginary companion.

I had come to Inverkirkaig in Sutherland wanting to climb Suilven. It is not one of Scotland's highest mountains, but it is certainly one of its noblest. A fine majestic pillar rising out of the moorland, eight miles from any road. To climb it is a hard day's walk from any direction. But for me it had now become something rather more – a physical expression of my desire to reach "Horeb", to climb the "mountain of God" and my desire to hear the quiet whisper of a voice. The day contained a dramatic range of Scotland's weather, short of snow. I began and came home in sunshine. I saw no one all day. It was a demanding slog across bog and rocky ridges to reach the base, and a tiring steep scramble up scree and bracken to the saddle.

On the top of Suilven there was steady rain, a strong wind and the threat that cloud would envelop the whole ridge in a short while. There was wind and storm. No fire.

Did I hear the "gentle whisper of a voice"? Certainly all day I was in conversation with God – muttering about the bogs and my wet feet, exhilarating in wind and sun, reflecting on what I wanted life and ministry to be about "going forward," praying for family and friends. Maybe the point about the "whisper of a voice" is that you hear it without knowing you hear it. It shapes your thinking, your decisions, your future in ways you are not really aware of. Maybe it is a refining, a reshaping that takes place because you are there before the Living God, seeking to be open, seeking to listen - and deep within you "hear" and are changed. I know that the day climbing Suilven was decisive for my pilgrimage, and my desire to be shaped and directed by God, but I cannot find words to describe what happened that day.

Dramatic new directions opened up for Elijah –he was to cause two revolutions and anoint two new kings, and then appoint his successor, for his time was coming to an end. Perhaps we can suppose for the Magi, that with no star to guide, they were held to their purpose to find the new born King, by just such a "whisper of a voice" that kept them going forward, kept them hungry, full of desire to meet the King.

Kenneth Steven is a contemporary Scottish poet. He writes well of how place and pilgrimage, in very down to earth ways, can be critical for the encounter with God. He is also able to capture the sense of "unfulfilled fulfilment" that is the heart of pilgrimage – the need to keep coming back, satisfied yet unsatisfied. This poem is from his Iona focused collection:

IONA

Is this place really nearer to God?
Is the wall thin between our whispers
And his listening? I only know
The world grows less and less –
Here what matters is conquering the wind,
Coming home dry-shod, getting the fire lit.
I am not sure whether there is no time here
Or more time, whether the light is stronger
Or just easier to see. That is why
I keep returning, thirsty, to this place
That is older than my understanding,
Younger than my broken spirit.

(from Iona: Poems, 2000, see for his books: kennethsteven.co.uk)

The Magi's hidden journey

The journey of the Magi was long enough for the questions and doubts to arise. The most likely reading of Matthew's text would suggest that the star they had seen at home, did not appear again until it guided them on the final part of their journey from Jerusalem to Bethlehem (perhaps confirming the planetary conjunction theory!). Contrary to the suggestion of our Christmas cards, they did not follow the star night by night across the tranquil desert. They travelled without a guide, still motivated by the experience they had shared on the banks of the Tigris, drawn by the gentle whisper of a voice just beyond hearing, still holding to the conviction that a truly significant King of the Jews had been born. Perhaps sometimes doubting, sometimes just struggling on, thinking this had all been a gigantic miscalculation, folly. And what would they do when they got there?

They would have travelled through village and town, beside rivers and canals, sometimes in the bustle, often alone with their thoughts on long days. They would have come up through the barren and dangerous Judean desert to the obvious place to find a newly born heir to the Jewish throne – Jerusalem.

Journey and pilgrimage are common metaphors today for our lives – but even so we often forget the potential for change, growth and encounter that daily life offers. Iona, Taizé, Jerusalem, Santiago may help but daily life also can have the possibilities of pilgrimage if we are alert to seeking, watching, listening and praying.

Pilgrimage in the Christian life has, perhaps, two essential dimensions. Like the Magi, for most of us, the journey to Christ is often long, tortuous, possessing its moments of revelation and insight, but also the long persevering when there is no star to guide. But beyond that meeting, that decisive encounter with Christ, there is the ongoing pilgrimage journey, the seeking and desiring, the desert and wilderness, the mountain top with its exhilaration, the temptations and darkness, the joy of finding.

> Hear my voice when I call, O Lord,
> be merciful to me and answer me.
> My heart says of you, 'Seek his face!'
> Your face Lord I will seek.
> Do not hide you face from me.
>
> (Psalm 27: 7-9)

In Bethlehem, whilst I was preparing and researching for this book, I met Dr Samy Awad, director of the Holy Land Trust. We were talking about the work of his organisation, but he then told me that in the Millennium year, 2000, at the height of the second Intifada, when emotions throughout the Middle East were running very high, he had been part of a re-enactment of the Journey of the Magi. This was called The Journey of the Magi 2000: A Pilgrimage for Peace. It had attempted through a re-enactment of the Magi's journey to awaken people in the divided and embittered lands of the Middle East to the millennium celebration of the birth of Christ and to demonstrate the healing, reconciliation and hope that his coming had brought. Messages about peace and reconciliation between nations and peoples, a spirit of generosity and hospitality, vulnerability, forgiveness were woven through the whole venture.

Sami put me in touch with Dr Robin Wainwright who had planned the pilgrimage over an eight-year period, and then led it. Dr Wainwright wrote a reflection, for which I am grateful, on the experience and has made his pictures and other material available to me. I find his report and the original venture a remarkable reflection on the significance of the original story, and a very powerful re-interpretation for the contemporary world.

WALKING THROUGH A SACRED WINDOW

Dr. Robin Wainwright

Our motive for creating our pilgrimage initially came from a desire to protest against the horrors and futility of social violence and war. My wife and I were distraught about the war with Iraq in 1991. For instance, the carpet-bombing that took place in the south of Iraq fell on villages of Chaldean Christians, but seemingly no Christians in the West knew they were there, or cared. So how does one get people in the West to see invisible strangers as people? This was when my wife and I came up with the idea of reenacting the original Journey of the Magi to honor Jesus, the Prince of Peace, on the second millennium of his birth. Our hope was that Christians in the West might discover through our pilgrimage that there were members of the Christian family all along our way, in Iraq, Syria, Jordan and Palestine. It would also be an opportunity to introduce people to Muslim believers who greatly respect Jesus, and who are worthy of our respect. As the Apostle Paul admonishes us, "Whenever we have the opportunity, we should do good to all people, especially to those in the family of faith" (Galatians 6.10)

Our intention was to travel on foot and camel, following in the footsteps of the Magi along their original 1200 mile route, from Iraq to Bethlehem. In keeping with the One, called The Prince of Peace, we would be unarmed, and solely depending on the Grace of God and the acceptance and hospitality of the people we encountered on the way.

Our mission would be to pray a blessing upon all the people—on their houses, and families, and animals and fields—and for God's Peace upon their lives. In short, we saw the year 2000 as a moment of kairos—a sacred window of time—when extraordinary things might be possible. Thus was born The Journey of the Magi 2000: A Pilgrimage for Peace.

As we began to share our idea with others, we were met with an almost unanimous response: not only would such a pilgrimage be unwise, it would be impossible.
While the physical challenge could perhaps be overcome with strenuous preparation and effort, the political and social obstacles would certainly prove insurmountable. But with the encouragement of a small group of Palestinian Christians in Bethlehem, my wife and I spent the next eight years researching the original route of the Magi, and physically exploring the terrain by car, one section at a time, from Iraq to Bethlehem. During this time we also found teams of local people to own the project in each country. The enthusiasm for the idea of our pilgrimage from both local Christians and Muslims the entire length of the route gave us much needed encouragement.

STUMBLING OUT OF THE STARTING GATE

After all the years of diligent preparation, we grew in confidence that what some viewed as a crazy idea could be done successfully. We had mapped out a carefully planned schedule of how many miles we would travel each day, and where we would pitch tents for the entire two months of our pilgrimage. In early October our team of 12 pilgrims from many different countries, representing Christians from around the world, traveled in two vans for 10 hours across the huge desert expanse between Amman, Jordan and Baghdad, Iraq. Once we were settled into our hotel, we began working out final arrangements to get underway. We would depart from Ctisiphon, on the eastern bank of the Tigris River, one day south of Baghdad. Ctisiphon had been the western capital of the Parthian empire, and the Magi, who served the royal families of Parthia, would have departed from there.

Then we got a call from the Iraqi authorities. They were concerned about our safe passage, and our Pilgrimage for Peace was being put on hold indefinitely. Back in mid-July, the Second Intifada had erupted in Jerusalem, and was growing worse day by day. The programing on Iraqi state television mostly consisted of martial music, and announcements of how many Iraqi volunteers had signed up to go liberate Palestine, and throw the Israelis into the sea. It looked like 8 years of planning was going down the drain.

After many days of prayer and frantic negotiating, we were finally given a limited approval to engage in our pilgrimage "for four or five days", after which it was advised that we should go home. Even this small window of grace was only possible due to the intervention of our local Iraqi support group of Assyrian Christians. We were especially indebted to the labors of General George Sada, the highest ranked Christian in the Iraqi air force, and a member of the large Presbyterian church in Baghdad. General Sada had access to the highest levels of the Iraqi security apparatus, and literally put his career and possibly his life on the line in his efforts to secure permission for us to get underway

TRAVELING THROUGH IRAQ

On Sunday, October 22, we departed from Ctisiphon and crossed the Tigris River on a make-shift pontoon bridge. All the fixed bridges across the Tigris had been destroyed in 1991. On the west bank of the Tigris, we traveled north to Kohe, the site of the oldest dedicated Christian church in the world, established in 70 A.D by a follower of one of Jesus's original 12 disciples. To our surprise a large gathering of Eastern Orthodox Christians were waiting for us there, to pray a blessing upon us and send us on our way. Then we traveled west to the Euphrates River and proceeded north.

The Iraqi government was very mistaken in their fears about the reception we would receive from the Iraqi people. By this time, Iraqi state television was announcing that millions of volunteers had signed up to liberate Palestine, but truth be told, I think most Iraqis understood that the only people going to Palestine were our humble little group of pilgrims. We had managed to announce on Iraqi radio and television that, in preparing to honor Jesus on Christmas day, 2000 A.D., we would be praying a blessing on each home and field that we passed on the way to Bethlehem. So along our way we found red carpets placed out on the road, welcoming us into their home to share tea, and to pray a blessing upon them and their household. So many, that on some days it was hard to fulfill the miles we had set for the day.

Families came up to us and placed coins in our hands. "Please take this to a Palestinian family, they need it more than we do", they said. There was a special moment as we passed through Falluja that will always stand out in my mind. Standing back from the road was an old woman dressed all in black. Her teeth were missing. She had her hand raised above her head and was crying out at the top of her voice, repeating the same phrase over and over, but my Arabic was not good enough to understand what she was saying. She seemed scary, and I thought maybe she was calling out a curse upon us. So I asked one of our Iraqi guides, "what is the old woman saying?" He said, "she is saying, 'God bless the womb who bore you!'" I was humbled. We had come to Iraq with the intention of giving a blessing. Here in Falluja, in the heart of Sunni tribalism, we were receiving one.

By this time, due to the enthusiastic reception we were receiving, the Iraqi government had decided that we would be allowed to continue our pilgrimage as planned all the way up to the border with Syria. We began each day on our pilgrimage with a simple spiritual discipline. Each day we would travel using one of the 99 beautiful names of God as our focus. These are the names that Muslims recite with their string of prayer beads. But they are names familiar to Christians as well, as most are found in our Bible as well as in the Koran. We would gather in a circle together, Muslims and Christians, and read a passage from Scripture in both Arabic and English. Then we would have a short meditation based on the name of God we traveled under that day, and at the conclusion, we would call out, "walk and pray", and off we would go.

There were long stretches of desert road where there were no villages at all. On these days we would concentrate on praying for the Peace of God over Iraq, whose people had been suffering under war and deprivation since 1980. On our final full day in Iraq, walking the last 20 miles through the border city Al Qaim, something extraordinary happened. Part of our support team in Iraq included six Shiite camel drivers, who came from the holy Shiite city of Najaf. As the day began, they came to us and asked if they could have the three staffs we carried. They were shaped like a shepherd's crook and fashioned into a cross. They went before us carrying the three crosses, while one of them chanted in Arabic from the Gospel of John. They continued this all day until we arrived at the border. Once again we were humbled beyond words.

TRAVELING THROUGH SYRIA

As we crossed into Syria, we had to get new camels and camel drivers. They were supplied to us by one of the Bedouin tribes from the historic oasis city of Palmyra, who also managed all our logistics throughout Syria in superb fashion. On Friday, November 10th, we arrived at Dura Europas on the west bank of the Euphrates River. This was the place where the Magi would have crossed over by boat from the east bank of the Euphrates on their way to Palmyra. After a day's rest, we left the road and traveled west for several days across the desert, following the original route of the Magi to Palmyra.

We entered Palmyra in the evening just before sunset. A large crowd of people followed with us through the town. As it happened, this night was the beginning of Ramadan, and it is traditional for rulers to release some prisoners on the occasion. Just at dark our parade of pilgrims was met by a large number of prisoners from a nearby prison, who were walking into town in the opposite direction. One particular prisoner caught my eye. He was severely physically impaired, perhaps from cerebral palsy. But he was limping his way straight toward me. The other prisoners began to hit him about the head and shout at him, trying to deter him from getting near me. I was all dressed in white, to identify me as someone on a sacred journey, and perhaps they thought it was wrong for such a deformed person to approach me. But he would not be turned back. Despite repeated blows to the head he fought his way to reach me. I think he desperately wanted to get a blessing from the pilgrim. I embraced him and spoke an Arabic blessing in his ear. Then the crowd of prisoners surged past me and he was gone. I have often thought that this encounter may have been one of the most important moments of the whole journey.

Several days later we reached Damascus. One of our pilgrims, Peter Thiep, went to the outdoor market to get supplies. Across a table of vegetables he spotted another young man who had markings on his forehead indicating that he was from Peter's own Nuer tribe in Sudan. They talked and discovered that they had actually gone to school together in the same village. The young man was part of a group of Catholic Christians who had escaped the violence in Sudan, and were now refugees there in Damascus. There were a total of 60 men, women and children. That night we invited all of them to dinner, and heard their stories of hardship and faith. When we left Damascus several days later, eight of their men joined our pilgrimage for the next seven days until we reached the border with Jordan.

We had now been following in the footsteps of the Magi for more than five weeks. During this time, the violence associated with the Second Intifada in Palestine-Israel had continued to grow. For several years leading up to the year 2000, many different Christian organizations had sought to arrange to have a role in the festivities in Bethlehem associated with the 2000th anniversary of Jesus' birth. But as the violence increased, they one by one began to cancel. But we had come too far to turn back now. We were going to be there on Christmas Day no matter what.

FROM JORDAN TO PALESTINE

The first couple days in Jordan we had rain showers, and as we crossed up over the hills of Gilead it actually began to snow. A week later we arrived at the baptismal site of Jesus, located as it says in the Gospel of John, "east of the Jordan River" (John 1.28). We spent an extra day there in prayer, giving thanks for our safe passage of nearly 1200 miles. We also held a foot washing service to honor the four Jordanian camel drivers who had served us so graciously from the Jordan border to the border with Israel, even though this meant a special hardship for them. They were keeping the fast during Ramadan, and they traveled all day long without eating or drinking water.

Unfortunately, at 3 A.M. the next morning I woke up violently ill, and I was unable to continue with the group. My wife and I stayed at a hotel by the Dead Sea while I recuperated, and our pilgrims went on without us. They walked out to the Allenby Bridge to cross the no-man's land between Jordan and Israel. Special arrangements had been made by our Palestinian partners to allow the group to walk across. Some of us had walked the entire way from Ctisiphon in Iraq, and we wanted to walk the remaining miles to Bethlehem.

At about 9 O'clock that night we heard a knock on our door. When we opened the door we were shocked to see two of our four wise men standing there. They were black Africans, from Zimbabwe and Sudan, and they had been turned back at the border control with Israel. So they had to find their way back across the no-man's land, which takes two separate buses--one from the Israeli passport control to the transfer point in the middle of the no-man's land, and then a second bus from the transfer point to the Jordanian passport control. After reentering Jordan, they then had to walk around to our hotel.

The next morning my wife called the American Embassy in Israel and got an American woman on the phone who happened to be black. She was outraged, and promised to make calls to government officials and media outlets. A member of our Jordanian support team was a well-known Palestinian journalist, with numerous published articles in prestigious U.S. newspapers such as the New York Times. He began calling his contacts at the Associated Press and other news outlets in the U.S. By nightfall the story of our two black wise men being turned back at the Israeli border on their way to honor Jesus in Bethlehem was threatening to become something of a diplomatic embarrassment for Israel. Miraculously, by the next morning I was recovered enough to continue the journey. Equally miraculous, our two African Magi were invited by Israeli authorities to by all means come over and join the rest of our group.

CHRISTMAS DAY IN BETHLEHEM

Back in 1996 we had worked with local Christians to establish in Bethlehem a new organization, Holy Land Trust, to serve the community and the search for peace. We hired a Palestinian Christian named Sami Awad to lead the work, and take on the perhaps impossible task of making it possible for our humble Journey of the Magi to be part of the celebrations on Christmas Day, 2000 A.D. in Manger Square. Due to the amazing work of Sami and Holy Land Trust, our humble pilgrimage had become the main event on Christmas day, 2000 A.D. in Bethlehem.

The last miles of our journey began late in the afternoon on Christmas day at a church in Shepherds Field. A Muslim peace organization had joined with Holy Land

Trust to put together a torch parade for peace that would follow our four wise men on camels three winding miles up the road to Manger Square. Thousands of people participated, Muslims and Christians together, making a serpentine line of torches as wide as the road and the whole three miles long. Thousands more stood on balconies and rooftops along the route, singing and waving and calling out to us. In Manger Square a crowd of seven thousand people awaited our arrival. Holy Land Trust had built a stage there, where a dance troop and singers from Nazareth presented a pageant play of the Christmas story, with colorful costumes and wonderful music. And at just the right moment, our four Magi arrived on their camels in regal costumes to present their gifts to Joseph and Mary and the baby Jesus.

As stated at the beginning, we saw the year 2000 as a moment of kairos—a sacred window of time—when extraordinary things might be possible. Much of our success in completing this pilgrimage and arriving in Manger Square on Christmas night was due to the fact that, despite all the tensions throughout the region that occurred with the outbreak of the Second Intifada, many Muslims viewed the moment in the same way, and gave our Journey of the Magi 2000: Pilgrimage for Peace a special dispensation to do things that would normally be impossible. We had indeed walked through a sacred window.

FINAL REFLECTIONS

Some of our original goals went unfulfilled. The Second Intifada completely overwhelmed our attempts to broadcast our pilgrimage in the West. Our message of a Pilgrimage for Peace could not break through the noise of war. However, throughout the Middle East millions of Muslims, not only in Iraq and Syria, but in Lebanon, Jordan, and the Gulf states, heard the news that in seeking to honor Jesus on His 2000th birthday, a group of Christians were traveling from Iraq to Bethlehem on foot and camel, praying for peace, and praying a blessing on all on the way. Hopefully, this provided for some in the Middle East an alternative narrative concerning Christians.

Despite all our earnest prayers for peace for the people in Iraq and Syria, life has become far more difficult and dangerous for them than we could have ever imagined. Our hearts are broken over the suffering that has been visited upon them through violence and war.

We suspect that it will be decades before any pilgrims for peace might follow in our footsteps and repeat our reenacting of the Journey of the Magi.

Holy Land Trust has gone on to be an important community organization in Palestine. It has a large staff of Christians and Muslims working together to serve the needs of the community. HLT has provided training in non-violence in over 60 Muslim villages throughout Palestine. It works closely with Israeli peace groups on various projects in the West Bank, such as rebuilding houses in cooperation with Rabbis Against Home Demolitions. HLT has had over 600 people spend their summer in Bethlehem, learning the principles of non-violence, and serving the people of Palestine. A link to their program can be found at Palestine Summer.org. In May of 2015, Sami Awad will be awarded an Honorary Doctorate of Letters Degree by Chicago Theological Seminary, on the 50th anniversary of this award having been presented to Dr. Martin Luther King. .

Reflecting on the Millennium Pilgrimage

I was moved to hear of this re-enactment of the Magi's journey to Bethlehem, not least because of the eight years it took to plan, the very real risks and dangers that it involved, and the surrounding political complexities. Risk, danger and political complexity were part of the first Magi's experience. In other ways the 2000 Magi Pilgrimage was able to give expression to the messages that could only be guessed at, tentatively anticipated by the Magi.

The 2000 Pilgrimage gave vivid expression to the radical inclusiveness that the call of the Magi first signalled. They were called – religious, cultural and linguistic outsiders – to give literal human expression to the dawning fulfilment of the blessing of the nations through the descendants of Abraham. So, this modern pilgrimage consisting of Americans and Europeans, a Sudanese, a Zimbabwean, Palestinians, assisted by Syrians and Iraqis, demonstrates the new, redeemed and diverse community that is God's purpose, and demonstrates it right in the heart of countries characterized by narrowing factionalism, sectarianism and strife.

Travelling through volatile lands at the height of the Second Intifada, they demonstrated that these lands are the birthplace and the homeland of Jesus, and affirmed the place that Christians have held in local communities over many centuries – and this at a time when they felt under threat, their future uncertain. This situation is one that is even more desperate and acute today, as the very existence of Christian communities in these lands is in doubt.

For the 2000 Pilgrimage travellers, the heart of their vision was the offering of gifts. As the Magi had laid their treasures at the feet of the Christ Child, so they wished to share the gifts and treasure of Christ with the communities through which they passed. The gifts they brought were the desire to give and receive hospitality, to offer reconciliation for the hurts of history, to build small bridges of new understanding and relationship, to demonstrate the welcome of the Prince of Peace.

As they travelled these could only be hints, but since 2000, through various channels, including the Holy Land Trust headed by Dr Sami Awad, more practical and substantial programmes have developed such as the programme to rebuild Palestinian homes demolished by the Israeli authorities, carried out in collaboration with the Israeli organisation Rabbis Against Home Demolition.

The Magi in the House of Herod; James Tissot; Brooklyn Museum , NY

CHAPTER 5

DANGEROUS ENCOUNTERS

Matthew Chapter 2:

> **1** After Jesus was born in Bethlehem in Judea, during the time
> of King Herod, Magi from the east came to Jerusalem **2** and
> asked, "Where is the one who has been born king of the Jews?
> We saw his star when it rose and have come to worship him."
> **3** When King Herod heard this he was disturbed, and all
> Jerusalem with him. **4** When he had called together all the
> people's chief priests and teachers of the law, he asked them
> where the Messiah was to be born. **5** "In Bethlehem in Judea,"
> they replied, "for this is what the prophet has written:
>
> > **6** "'But you, Bethlehem, in the land of Judah,
> > are by no means least among the rulers of Judah;
> > for out of you will come a ruler
> > who will shepherd my people Israel.'"

7 Then Herod called the Magi secretly and found out from them the
exact time the star had appeared. **8** He sent them to Bethlehem and said,
"Go and search carefully for the child. As soon as you find him, report
to me, so that I too may go and worship him."

Arrival in Jerusalem

Very probably the route of the Magi's caravan took them across the broad valley of the Euphrates and the Tigris, on across the Jordanian and Syrian deserts and down into the valley of the Jordan River, across the river, past Jericho, and then up the long harsh desert road to Jerusalem. If the (speculative) suggestion is correct that they were responding to the conjunction of Jupiter and Saturn, this may well have been in early December of 7BC. "A cold coming we had of it. . . ."

Feigning Faith

Herod the King,
'Racially Arab,
religiously Jewish,
culturally Greek,
politically Roman.'

Baffled, bewildered,
by naive strangers,
Shocked and scared,
by sacred page.
Secretly, exactly,
gathers facts,
feigns faith,
requests report:
Diligent intelligence.

Reaching the crest, with the desert behind them they would have looked down over the gardens of olive trees and the ancient cemeteries to the walls of Jerusalem, and the magnificent, though still unfinished, walls and sanctuaries of the Temple that King Herod was building. They had arrived! The dangers of the journey were behind them.

Dangerous Pilgrimage

Pilgrimage always has its dangers. In ancient times, of course, there were always the possibilities of attack and robbery on the way. Jesus' story of the Good Samaritan (Luke 10: 30) indicates the dangers of this last stretch of the journey up to Jerusalem. But there were other perils to be faced in the space between departure and arrival.

The empty spaces, the solitude and silence, even in the company of others, gives time for the unfinished business of the soul to rise to the surface – fears, insecurities, anxieties and guilt that we thought had been dealt with long ago. The loss of our daily frameworks, patterns and habits, the disciplines provided by family or professional life, make us vulnerable to our inner selves, to an unexpected rawness and fear. It can be an emotionally turbulent time. We can suppress it, force it back where it came from to continue its destructive work, or we can bring it into the light for acknowledgement and healing. On pilgrimage, the journey is as much the place of meeting with God as is the moment of arrival, if we will let it be. It can be a time of darkness as well as light, night and day. The danger, the temptation, is to avoid the realisation that *this* is, at least in part, what we came for. It is not a distraction, it is the real thing, it is the goal of our pilgrimage in some measure – though we may feel that our purpose and our hopes are collapsing around us.

> Then the camel men cursing and grumbling
> And running away, and wanting their liquor and women,
> And the night fires going out , and the lack of shelters,
> And the cities hostile and the towns unfriendly
> And the villages dirty and charging high prices;
> A hard time we had of it.
> At the end we preferred to travel all night,
> Sleeping in snatches.
> With the voices singing in our ears, saying
> That this was all folly.
>
> (T S Eliot The Journey of the Magi)

At such moments, though we are "on pilgrimage", we can lose all momentum, we can cease to journey. Vision can evaporate and we can forget the goal of our travelling. The star no longer guides. We have no idea whether any of this beset our Magi as they persevered and eventually came in sight of their goal, but they were on an expedition into uncharted personal and spiritual territory that must have involved doubt, anxiety and the fear that "this was all folly."

Dangers in Jerusalem

But in fact their greatest dangers, the greatest threat to their journey lay just ahead. In Jerusalem.

Any pilgrim visit to Jerusalem today is almost certain to begin with the panoramic view from the Mount of Olives, possibly the first view of the Magi, though there are a number of gates, now as then, into the Holy City. The view is spectacular. Though Jerusalem is on a hill, it is lower than several neighbouring hills and you can see right over the walls and into the city. It is, even today, a surprisingly small and compact settlement – though it was even smaller in Jesus' time. Today's walls were mostly build by the Ottoman Turks in the 16th century and subsequently, but they give a startling impression of the city that Jesus knew. Crowning it all, then and now - was a religious shrine of great beauty that holds the eye and draws it back time and time again. Then it was Herod's Temple, nearing completion, and already recognised as one of the great sights of the Roman world.
Today, of course, on the same site is the Dome of the Rock, one of the most peerless buildings ever constructed, with its glittering gilded dome, constructed by the Umayyad caliph, Abd al-Malik, and completed in 691. Like Herod's Temple and like many of the great religious buildings it is an ambiguous building, speaking of power, pride and authority as well as spiritual aspiration.

Today we go on pilgrimage to the "Holy Land" and to the "Holy City" – a city, we are told, sacred to three Faiths. So it is, but it is, like the Temple, ambiguous. In Scripture it is a place of both holiness and deep wickedness, of faith and rampant rebellion, a dangerous place for those on pilgrimage.

It was the city of David, the centre of Israel's royal and Messianic hope, but also the place where those aspirations could be most cruelly betrayed:

> Therefore this is what the LORD, the God of Israel, says, "I am going to bring such disaster on Jerusalem and Judah that the ears of everyone who hears of it will tingle...I will wipe out Jerusalem as one wipes out a dish, wiping it and turning it upside down."
>
> (II Kings 21:12-13)

Jesus himself paused during his triumphal entry into Jerusalem prior to his betrayal, trial and crucifixion and wept over the city, an event still commemorated at the Dominus Flevit church on the Mount of Olives:

> As he approached Jerusalem and saw the city, he wept over it and said, "If you, even you, had only known on this day what would bring you peace – but now it is hidden from your eyes. The days will come upon you when your enemies will build an embankment against you and encircle you and hem you in on every side. They will dash you to the ground, you and your children within your walls. They will not leave one stone on another, because you did not recognise the time of God's coming to you."
>
> (Luke 19: 41-44)

"You did not recognise the time of God's coming to you." And what was true of the Triumphal Entry and the subsequent events of Holy Week, were equally true as the Magi came down maybe the very same hill in search of an audience with Herod, Rome's appointed King of the Jews.

Herod was one of the most extraordinary, terrifying and gifted rulers of the ancient world. In the words of the New Testament scholar, Kenneth Bailey, "he was racially Arab, religiously Jewish, culturally Greek and politically Roman."[viii] Herod's father was from an Arab tribe in Idumea (he was an Edomite in Old Testament terms) from south of Judea, beyond Beersheba. His mother was Jewish, from Petra. He moved, as self-interest and self-preservation demanded, between Jewish and Graeco-Roman religion, always with a view to his survival and his relationship with Rome. Whilst building the Temple in Jerusalem, he was involved in building grand temples to Pan and other Greek deities in Caesarea Philippi. He was one of the great builders of the ancient world. Evidence of his colossal and skilfully constructed building survives in many places, notably at the Western Wall of the Temple Mount and at the Tomb of Abraham in Hebron.

He ruled Judea as "King of the Jews" under Roman authority from 37BC until his death in 4BC. He was brutal, fearful and insecure. He built the massive fortress on the mountain at Masada as a refuge, but as far as we know never visited it. He murdered as many remnants of the Jewish Hasmonean dynasty that had preceded him as he could get his hands on. He murdered many of his real or perceived enemies, his beloved wife, Mariamne, and her mother, and several of his own sons. On his deathbed, to ensure that his death would evoke mourning somewhere, he arranged for many of the Jewish notables to be assembled in the hippodrome in Jericho and killed when his

death was announced. Fortunately for them, this was not carried out.
This was the man with whom the Magi now sought an audience.

"Where is the one born King of the Jews?"

So it is not hard to imagine the atmosphere generated by the Magi's question. It was doubtless asked in all innocence, for, surely, this was the house of the King of the Jews? Were the Magi expecting to find a young child in the house of Herod?
Did they somehow suspect that something larger, more universally significant, was afoot? Either way, the question met with a bemused response: "No baby king here!" and the atmosphere chilled. For Herod, however, the phrase "King of the Jews" had other overtones. This was a title for the Messiah, a far more threatening possibility even than some rival child-king. Was there some new Messianic movement out there, unknown to Herod and his security forces? No wonder that Herod "was disturbed, and all Jerusalem with him." "Jerusalem" was doubtless disturbed for fear of Herod's notoriously suspicious nature and his capacity for murderous cruelty. Yes, Jerusalem was disturbed, and with the city, the chief priests and the teachers of the law that Herod now summoned for advice.

"Where is the Messiah to be born," he asked. The answer was not difficult, well known to those professionally concerned to know the Scriptures. For this is what the prophet says:

> But you, Bethlehem, in the land of Judah, are by no means least among the rulers of Judah, for out of you will come a ruler who will be the shepherd of my people Israel. (Matt 2:6)

Thus Matthew, but he has, however, adapted the famous text in a number of ways. The verse quoted by the priests and teachers of the law is, essentially, Micah 5:2, but with the final phase borrowed from II Samuel 5:2: "You shall shepherd my people Israel, and you shall become their ruler."
This slight amendment strengthens the reference of the quotation to the line of David, which Matthew has so strongly underlined in Ch.1, as well as to the shepherding role of the Messiah, so warmly expressed in the ministry of Jesus. Other changes are less significant, with the exception of the change from Bethlehem being described as "small" (in the Old Testament version of Micah) or "least" (in the Septuagint) to "by no means least." This change in Matthew's mind is no doubt associated with the new importance that Bethlehem now has as the actual birthplace of the Messiah. This dramatic piece of information is still hidden from everyone in Herod's throne room.

So the Magi have the precise information they need to proceed on their quest for the King of the Jews. However, before we accompany them on the final five or six miles of their journey south to Bethlehem, some further reflection is needed.

It is Scripture that leads us to Christ

Matthew's overarching purpose, as he begins his Gospel, is accurately to identify and locate the unlikely figure of Jesus of Nazareth as the Messiah, as the son of David and the fulfilment of the promises to Abraham, and to demonstrate the wide inclusive nature of the good news that Jesus embodies. The Magi are a startling example of just that.

They began their quest, unknowingly, at the call of God, discerning it within the tangled complexities of their astrological systems, and within their world view and its assumptions. They set off to search for the newborn "King of the Jews" not knowing what that title really meant, who it belonged to, or where he might be found. Their search has brought them into some very dangerous company, but it is the context in which the witness of God's Word can be discovered. It is here that the crucial revelation takes place that enables them to continue successfully and with increasing joy to their destination. With the direction of Scripture, and with the Star again making its appearance, they can find the One for whom they search. The Star brought the Magi to the Scriptures, and the Scriptures will bring them to Christ.

For the Magi, Jerusalem was a crucial part of the jigsaw. But the custodians of Jerusalem's heritage, faith, scriptures and worship – the king, the priests and the teachers of the law – cannot receive the witness of Scripture. They know it, can quote it, but are in rebellion against it, and are deaf to it. The outsiders are ignorant of it, but receive the Word of God; the insiders know it but cannot receive it. The warning to everyone who might consider themselves an insider is plain. Neither the "power" of the King, nor the "wisdom" of the clergy can comprehend or receive the truth in the Christ Child. The vulnerable ignorance of the Magi renders them open to God's grace and leading. This is echoed a number of times through Matthew's Gospel:

> At that time Jesus said, "I praise you, Father, Lord of heaven and earth, because you have hidden these things from the wise and learned, and revealed them to little children. Yes, Father, for this was your good pleasure." (Matt 11:25-6)

And we may suppose that Matthew understood this as fulfilled in the ongoing life of the fragile Christian communities he knew in Palestine and Syria in the traumatic social and political conditions that prevailed after the fall of Jerusalem to Roman assault in 70AD.

The Magi, Herod and the Gospel

In his monumental commentary, Frederick Bruner encourages us to look at the encounter between the Magi and Herod in one further way[ix]. He writes:

> It is only when we learn to see ourselves in the problematic people of the Gospel – from the four questionable couples in the genealogy, through the Magi. . . and now Herod, to the Pharisees, Romans and failing disciples at the passion – that we will be reading the Gospel existentially.

He continues to explain that the Gentile Magi describe what we all are in an external sense: aliens, "aliens from the commonwealth of Israel and strangers to the covenants of promise, having no hope and without God in the world" (Eph 2:12). Herod, we could say, describes what we all are internally: rebels "following the desires of flesh and senses, (and so) by nature children of wrath, like everybody else" (Eph 2:3).

Like the Magi, Herod had a chance and a choice. There in his conference with the Magi and Jerusalem's religious leaders he heard the invitation to go to Bethlehem. The Magi hear and respond to the invitation. Herod sees the invitation only as a threat to be countered in some way. "His own did not receive him "(Jn 1: 11). If the Magi are an encouragement to faith that God's grace is for us, so Herod is a warning of what happens when grace is rejected. And, as the story of Herod so graphically illustrates, when that happens terrible hurt can be caused to the innocents around us.

We should not make the "tabloid press" mistake with Herod – so to demonise him that we no longer really regard him as human, and therefore not really as one of us. Herod, like the other "monsters" of human history is one of us. And the characteristics of his personality find their place in us, in society, and in the church – ambition, ruthlessness, self-centredness, greed, jealousy, cruelty. There is the narrowest of lines between his journey and that of the Magi.

Seekers or Spies?

As the interview concludes, Herod recruits his exotic visitors to his agenda. He urges them to continue their journey to Bethlehem, "Go and make a careful search for the child. As soon as you find him, report to me, so that I too may go and worship him."

The story is crisply told. We are left with no idea as to whether the Magi saw through Herod, mistrusted his intentions, or whether they were taken in by the welcome, the interest and the bonhomie. Either way, they have been neatly recruited as Herod's spies, to keep him informed of what would probably turn out to be of no account, but which could be quickly stamped on should it prove to be yet another subversive movement.
The star reappears, and the star-led pilgrim seekers and spies move on.

PART 2: WORSHIPING THE CHILD.

The Magi and the Child; He Qi; www.heqiart.com

Adoration of the Magi; James Tissot; Brooklyn Museum, NY

CHAPTER 6

WORSHIP: THE STILL CENTRE

Matthew, chapter 2:

> **9** After they had heard the king, they went on their way, and the star they had seen when it rose went ahead of them until it stopped over the place where the child was. **10** When they saw the star, they were overjoyed. **11** On coming to the house, they saw the child with his mother Mary, and they bowed down and worshiped him. Then they opened their treasures and presented him with gifts of gold, frankincense and myrrh.

A. BOWING OUR KNEE

The Adoration by the Magi; picture by Robin Wainwright

Star-led to Bethlehem

Offerings Presented

Away from home,
Mission accomplished:
It is finished.

Star trek over,
King discovered,
But not as they know it.

Rapturous joy,
Offerings unwrapped.

Mined mineral, for brilliant mind;
Sweet savour, for sense of spirit;
Balm of burial, for enwrapped body.

Warned and turned,
They follow the Way:
Another way home

Herod was paranoid about challenges to his position and rule. Any talk of a new King of the Jews, even a baby king, churned up his anxieties, fears and murderous intent. He sent the Magi off to complete their journey, recruited as his spies, "so that I too may go and worship him." Were they suspicious? We don't know. Later it is a dream that warns them not to return to Herod – maybe bringing their suppressed suspicions to the surface.

For the moment, they were exhilarated. They have a clear destination – Bethlehem , just 5 or 6 miles distant. And, joy of joys, that night as they are hurrying on their way, their star reappeared. They had not seen it since they originally trusted instinct and their astrological experience and set off on this mad adventure to find a new born King of the Jews. The Star had brought them to hear the prophetic Jewish Scriptures, and the Scriptures had pointed them to the King that they sought.

Their weary and emaciated camels bore them up the steep slopes to the hill top village of Bethlehem – a small settlement, stretched along a rocky ridge, looking one way to the fields of Judea, the other to the desert. It was a community with a distinguished story behind it – Bethlehem was after all the home town of Israel's greatest king – but now it was a humble agricultural village with little significance.

What does this star language mean? "The star. . . went ahead of them until it stopped over the place where the child was." We cannot tell. Certainly it is recounted from the position of the travellers, not from any science of astronomy. In some sense, however, it seemed to have "stopped" and to be drawing their attention to a particular house. It is hard to capture the exuberant excess of the Greek phrase here. "They rejoiced with exceeding great joy" seems rather stiff. "They were thrilled to bits" seems not quite to match the majesty and weight of the moment. They were here! *He* was here! The rash adventure, the long pilgrimage, had reached its climax. It was not folly. But it was certainly a million miles from what they had expected when they set off: a toddler in a modest house belonging to a young couple in a small town with a long faded reputation. There were no palaces, no retainers, no splendour, no local buzz of excitement. Just the evening round of activities of a family home, with everyone now rushing round to receive some very strange and unexpected visitors.

There is the natural human story to be told here: a young family, following the evening routines of looking after a toddler, getting the evening meal ready (why do we assume it was an evening or night-time visit?), settling the animals down for the night. There's a knock at the door, or perhaps, more likely, a noisy kerfuffle outside the house, that brings the Family, and neighbours, out to see what is going on. In the narrow street that winds along Bethlehem's long ridge, is a bedraggled caravan - weary, travel-stained travellers with their hungry-looking camels and perhaps a few retainers. How many are there of them? We think of three, but Matthew gives us no clue. Tradition has fixed on three, but other ancient stories suggest four or five, or even a dozen. Their arrival has caused a local sensation. Neighbours come out to get a good look, children run around excitedly, dogs bark. Such strange clothes! And they speak a language that is hard to understand, but clearly related to the Palestinian Aramaic that Bethlehemites spoke. The term "Aramaic" describes a family of languages widely used through west Asia over a period of 3000 years, and was the administrative language for the successive empires of the East – Assyria, Babylon and Persia. It is very possible that whilst Jesus and his family spoke a local Palestinian Aramaic, the Magi spoke a Mesopotamian dialect, and that, with effort, conversation was possible[x].

The strange visitors are welcomed in. Perhaps the evening meal is stretched, rather thinly, to include the awkward and slightly embarrassed arrivals.

The Quaker poet, U. A Fanthorpe, caught this moment in a lovely phrase:

> And this was the moment
> When a few farm workers and three
> Members of an obscure Persian sect

Walked haphazard by starlight straight
Into the kingdom of heaven.[xi]

"Walked haphazard by starlight." How well that captures the exploratory, uncertain but persevering journey of the Magi, and how such trusting adventuring brought them "straight into the kingdom of heaven." That is how God does things.

This alerts us to the larger story being told here. We are now at the heart of Matthew's first major story through which the significance of Jesus the Messiah, the God-with-us Saviour, is being laid out. So that we do not domesticate, or nationalise the story, he has chosen a very disturbing narrative to engage us first of all. This story has already brought surprise, shock perhaps, the overthrowing of expectations. If you are going to follow *this* Messiah, you are going to have to think and live in some surprising new ways. This is a radical new way of seeing the course of Jewish history and expectation, a revolutionary way of looking at the world out there – the world of empire, and power, of ruthlessness, cruelty and fear.

And there is more to come. . . the second half of the chapter, when the Magi have departed, will concern a desperate family struggle to protect and preserve the young Child on whom so much depends. There will be no royal dignity here, no pomp and circumstance, only a desperate family fleeing for their lives. What kind of Son of Abraham, Son of David is this? If God is in this, what does it say about him, what kind of God he is?

But this is the centre of the story. If the artists and the Christmas illustrators have often got the first part of the story wrong, and ignored the last part, this they have often got right. Many artists have caught the wonder, the stillness, the utter focus and attention as the Magi kneel and offer the treasures they have brought – for whom they knew not when they set out. In a chapter full of journeys, dangers, dreams and drama, there is this still moment – the moment that reveals what all the journeying, seeking, persevering is all about. We don't want to hurry through this moment.

This is the still centre to which Matthew wants to draw us. This chapter illustrates the necessary journey of all Christian people. *Called* in a great diversity of ways according to God's grace from within our own world and culture with its beauties and values, but also its corruption and error, *led* to seek the One who alone is the answer to all our longing and seeking, *persevering* through all kinds of distractions, temptations and difficulties, and coming at last to the feet of the One God has sent, Jesus the Saviour, Immanuel, earth's true Lord, to *worship*. This scene, this tableau, which we know so well, where the Magi bow, worship, and offer of their treasures is a resonant and luminous portrayal of our destination as followers and seekers after Jesus, the place to which we came once decisively, and to which we return frequently, a place of homecoming, of welcome, nurture, self-offering and dedication. Let us enter the house thoughtfully, reverently, expectant. This scene is the first example of a community of people gathered at the feet of Jesus to worship. Some few decades later it is what happened in Matthew's small Syrian / Palestinian house church. It is what happens when we gather today. The Magi did it first.

This chapter has been described as "the gospel in miniature"[xii]. God's abundant grace brings radical outsiders on a journey to Christ, through perils and dangers not dissimilar to those in John Bunyan's Pilgrim's Progress. Suffering and rejection will follow in the story, but here is the centre of Christian faith and devotion – worship at the feet of Jesus.

The upside down nature of the Gospel is very evident here. From the encounter with Herod to the end of the chapter, Matthew refers always to "the Child", rather than to "Jesus" or "Christ". From verse 8 to 23 the term "Child" is used nine times, and is the only term used for Jesus. The use of this term highlights the vulnerability of Jesus and his parents in highly dangerous circumstances. Apocryphal Gospels and indeed the Quran refer to the young Christ Child as having precocious and miraculous gifts. Not so Matthew. In these verses the Child Jesus is a vulnerable toddler and does not speak in the story. God has placed his new initiative of love towards his world in this infant life, placed within this young inexperienced little family, in dangerous times. There is an interesting echo of this later in Matthew's Gospel (18: 1-5).

> "I tell you the truth, unless you change and become like little children, you will never enter the kingdom of heaven. Therefore whoever humbles himself like this child is the greatest in the kingdom of heaven. And whoever welcomes a little child in my name welcomes me."

The final phrase, "And whoever welcomes a little child in my name welcomes me" seems to be perfectly illustrated in the Magi worship in the Bethlehem home, and, with it, we realise the profound spiritual offence committed in the physical and sexual abuse against children, that appears commonly in our news. The childhood of Jesus is not simply a necessary stage in his progress to adulthood, but is in itself a demonstration of the meaning of the incarnation and of the Gospel. In our Christmas celebrations, how might we might we appropriately worship the *Child* at the heart of our carols and nativity plays?

So, just as the Magi enter the house, in surprise and wonder, for this is the last thing they expected, so must we. And also like little children, if we are to enter the kingdom of heaven. Here the grown, worldly wise, men of influence, steeped in esoteric knowledge, bow before a child. To the Child we must come in worship, and none of these worldly trappings help or qualify us in the slightest.

Bowing in Worship

The Greek word used in this chapter, and elsewhere in Matthew's Gospel for worship and its various derivative forms is *proskynesis.* The word can be used in at least two different ways. It can be used to speak of the offering of homage in entirely human contexts, such as bowing before royalty. It can also be used to describe the worship due to God. It is a word that Matthew favours in his writing. Mark uses the term only once. Matthew uses it nine times in his Gospel in addition to the three occasions in this chapter. One notable use is in the story of the Temptations of Jesus in chapter 4. Jesus replies to the offer of worldly princely power from the devil with the words, "For it is written, 'Worship the Lord your God, and serve him only.'" Worship is reserved for God alone.

So, when Matthew here describes the Magi as bowing down and worshipping the Child, there can be little doubt that he wants us to understand that they are worshipping the Child as one worships God, not simply bowing before an infant king. He is, as we have already learned, Immanuel, God-with-Us. The word *proskynesis* has its roots in the idea of fully prostrating yourself in homage and worship. The Magi, in an extraordinary scene, if we reconstruct it in our mind's eye, as international travellers of some dignity, social standing and significance, enter a modest home in Bethlehem, and offer worship, prostrating themselves in total homage, before a toddler, a Child, whose significance they can only begin to comprehend. There is simplicity, a trust, directness and a wholeheartedness about this scene of worship that characterises Christian worship at its best.

The scene illuminates our individual journeys to the place of worship, and the journey of the churches and congregations to which we belong. But we need to keep in mind the wider context. To embed this in our consciousness is one of Matthew's prime aims. This handful of strange visitors, who somehow have got hold of what is really happening here, are the beginnings of the most fundamental revolution in human relations. They are the beginning of the fulfilment of the ancient prophecy that Abraham's offspring, his Son, will bring blessing to the nations. And here they come, in all their oddness, to the feet of the one who bears the blessing into the world. Maybe we can say that at this moment they become "kings" as they represent the kingdoms and nations of the world, and "wise men" as they have seen the Wisdom and the Truth of God.

> Arise, shine, for your light has come, and the glory of the Lord rises upon you.

See, darkness covers the earth, and thick darkness is over the peoples,
But the Lord rises upon you and his glory appears over you.
Nations will come to your light, and kings to the brightness of your dawn.
(Isaiah 6-: 1-3)

This is a vision that Jesus himself, later in the Gospel, picks up and gives to it his characteristic celebratory character:

> I say to you that many will come from the east and the west, and will take their places at the feast with Abraham, Isaac and Jacob in the kingdom of heaven.
>
> (Matthew 8:11)

B.OFFERING OUR TREASURE

Adoration of the Magi; Andreas Mantegna; Getty Museum, LA

> Then they opened their treasures and presented him with gifts of gold, and of incense and of myrrh. (Matt 2: 11)

They open their Treasures

The moment at which the Magi offer their gifts is the moment invariably captured in the world's artistic representations. Perhaps we can pause for some moments before possibly the earliest surviving such representation, the beautiful Ravenna mosaic of the 6th century, reproduced at the head of Chapter 2. In resplendent and characteristic Parthian dress, Melchior, Balthazar and Gaspar step forward, completely focused on the one they have sought so long, holding aloft handsome silver vessels containing their gifts.

Such lavish gift-giving was common in the 1st centuries BC and AD, and Matthew's readers would not have regarded the offering of "treasures" as unlikely or as a romantic garnish on the story. In 10-9 BC, only a few years before these events, Herod completed the construction of a major port on the Mediterranean coast, Caesarea Maritima.[xiii] According to Josephus, ambassadors and delegates came from many nations to congratulate Herod, bringing with them extravagant gifts. And we have already mentioned the event in AD 66 when "magi" princes accompanied Tiridates, king of Armenia, to offer homage to Nero and brought many expensive gifts.

From Biblical literature, it is the visit of the Queen of Sheba (in Arabia) to Solomon which has most resonance:

> When the queen of Sheba heard about the fame of Solomon and his relation to the name of the LORD, she came to test him with hard questions. Arriving at Jerusalem with a very great caravan - with camels carrying spices, large quantities of gold and precious stones – she came to Solomon and talked with him about all that she had on her mind.
>
> (I Kings 10:1-2)

Matthew's readers would have made the connection at once. Here was a representative of the Gentile nations coming to Solomon, *the son of David,* to seek wisdom, and bearing gifts of gold and spices. Her story was recalled thereafter as an example of the submission of the nations to the Messiah (Psalm 72: 10-11; Isaiah 60:5-6). She was a forerunner of what, for Matthew, was now unfolding in reality as the Gentile nations, represented by the Magi, came to worship the Messiah, son of David, son of Abraham.

Throughout Christian history, there has been speculation about the meaning of the gifts the Magi brought. At the most obvious level, gold, incense (or frankincense) and myrrh are expensive commodities such as guests might take when visiting royalty – and we may suppose that the Magi expected to find the answer to their quest in the house of Herod. Gold of course has always been a sign of wealth. Frankincense, only found in Southern Arabia and Somalia (probably "Punt" in biblical terms) was an expensive perfume, and was burned both at religious ceremonies and social gatherings. Frankincense and myrrh occur together several times in the Song of Songs with a social and cosmetic meaning:

> Who is this coming up from the desert like a column of smoke,
> perfumed with myrrh and (frank)incense
> made from all the spices of the merchant?
>
> Song of Songs 3:6 (also 4:6, 14)

Myrrh, specifically, was a rare cosmetic perfume and an appropriate gift for a king, or his wife!:

> Before a girl's turn came to go in to King Xerxes, she had to complete twelve months of beauty treatment prescribed for the women, six months with oil of myrrh, and six with perfumes and cosmetics.
>
> (Esther 2:12)

Many commentators have wanted to delve deeper to uncover the meaning of the three gifts. Irenaeus in the early second century was the first to suggest a meaning which has found widespread favour from that day to this. The gold, Irenaeus proposes, speaks of royalty, the frankincense of divinity (though others have suggested priesthood) and the myrrh speaks of death and burial – thus prophetically outlining the meaning of the life of the Child in Bethlehem. Whether or not this was Matthew's intention, such symbolic reflection can open up rich and helpful insights into the story of Christ.

Personally I have been more drawn to the more straightforward interpretations. Firstly, that these are, in 1st century terms, simply appropriate gifts for a king, and the Magi naturally brought them in their search for the King of the Jews. And secondly, that these three precious commodities are basic elements in the divination, occult practices and rituals associated with their work as Magi priests. They were offering the "tools of their trade" to the king who was the object of their search.

Beyond the appropriateness of lavish royal gifts, probably all else is speculation – though speculation not without reward. For Joseph and Mary, however, these were luxury gifts such as they would never have owned before.

A Ming Vase in Bethlehem?

I found myself at a loose end in London on a Saturday morning. And prompted by a review in the Guardian I decided to go to see the exhibition of Chinese Ming Dynasty treasures at the British Museum. It was a stunning display, but it was the final item in the catalogue that caught my eye:" The Adoration of the Magi" by Andrea Mantegna[xiv]. *The Adoration of the Magi??* What was that doing here? I contained my questions whilst I enjoyed the splendours of the exhibition. Then, at last, there it was – on the wall next to the exit to the bookshop and cafe. Six heads – the Holy Family and the three Magi crammed into a small space just 20 inches by 25 inches.

Why was it here in this exhibition? That was immediately evident. The eldest Magus, bears the gift of gold, contained in an exquisite Ming porcelain cup or small vase. It is beautifully rendered, clearly from an actual example – as a similar vessel in an adjoining cabinet makes plain. In the exhibition the painting serves to illustrate the growing cultural and commercial contact between China, the Middle East and Europe in the late 15th century. Such items were extremely rare in Europe at that time, and had possibly reached Italy as a gift from Muslim rulers in Egypt or the Levant who were beginning to receive luxury goods from China. The technique of making porcelain was unknown in Europe at that time and these extremely delicate, exquisitely decorated vessels were highly prized.

This was not the first rendering of the Adoration of the Magi by Andrea Mantegna (c. 1430 – 1506). This picture was painted around 1500, but he had painted an earlier picture of the same subject in about 1460. That was a more conventional portrayal, with a colourful and exotic procession sweeping down a hillside road to a cave, where the three travellers offer their gifts to a virgin and child surrounded by cherubs. They are most definitely Kings, and arrayed magnificently accordingly. One of the Magi Kings is black – one of the earliest portrayals of an African Magus in Italian art. More commonly in Italian art of the period, black figures had been included in the cluster of retainers and servants accompanying white Magi.

By the time of the 1500 painting (actually his third representation of the Adoration of the Magi, the second, a fresco in the Vatican, having been destroyed in a fire in the 18th century), Mantegna's artistic and theological understanding had developed radically.

The "Adoration" of 1500, or thereabouts, impacts us quite differently. Like many of Mantegna's surviving paintings it is quite small. No longer does the story of the Magi coming to the Christ Child evoke a sweeping, exotic and royal panoply. This picture is close-up, almost as if recorded by a telescopic lens. Six heads crowd the canvas, and we are drawn right in. As viewers we find ourselves completing the circle of worship around the Child. Only the Christ Child is shown completely. Mantegna was not the inventor of this "telephoto" technique of establishing immediacy and intimacy, which he developed vigorously throughout his life, but this is probably the most effective example.

The picture is dense with interpretation. The universality and inclusivity of the community that gathers in worship around Christ is richly explored here with a new freedom. The three Magi represent, as was commonly done, the three Ages of Man, Melchior in the foreground representing old age, Balthasar behind him representing the strength of adulthood, and Caspar the vigour of youth. All come to the feet of Christ. Here the Magi are not represented as kings – as they were in his first painting of the subject. They are well-dressed but not royally or lavishly.

However, in exploring the extraordinary revolution of the Gospel, bringing the whole of humanity from the fringes to worship Christ, Mantegna goes a lot further. The Three Magi represent the three continents known at the time. In the front, the old man Melchior represents Europe, and is the first to kneel. The high dome of his forehead emphasising the wisdom and the maturity of European culture! He is the embodiment of the sage.

From there on it gets more interesting. The second Magus is a Turk, representing Asia. He is dressed in typical Ottoman Turkish clothing of the era, perhaps has Semitic rather than Turkish features, but carries a characteristically Turkish incense holder (such as you can still buy in the Istanbul Grand Bazaar). This I find quite extraordinary. I don't know whether this representation had been used before in European art. Constantinople, the great Christian capital of the Byzantine Empire, the surviving rump of the Roman Empire, had fallen to the Ottoman Turks less than fifty years previously, in 1453. The Turks were Muslims, and culturally their roots were in distant reaches of East Asia. They represented a major religious and military threat to the whole of Europe, and Montegna here portrays them boldly as included in God's calling to worship Christ. I find the portrayal of this Turkish Magus very sympathetic.

The third figure, the young Caspar, is clearly an African. Our manger scenes and Christmas cards now commonly portray one of the Magi as an African, but this is a pioneering and rather disturbing innovation at the close of the 15th century. How would Montegna have encountered black Africans? Who might have been a model for this striking figure? One result of the Black Death, the bubonic plague that ravaged Europe (and large parts of the Middle East and Asia) in the mid-14th century was a grave shortage of labour. As a result there was a marked upsurge in the import of slaves into Western Europe – both black and white, either from Eastern Europe, or the slave markets of the Middle

East. So for the first time in many centuries, black Africans could be encountered as servants in rich houses, or labourers on agricultural estates, especially in the countries bordering on the Mediterranean. So we may reasonably assume that the model for Mantegna's black Magus was a slave. We can only imagine the jumble of conflicting thoughts that this painting set off in the minds of those who first saw it. A domestic slave, possibly, in Padua, Mantua or Venice, cities in which much of Mantegna's work was done, became the image of one of these pioneers of response to the Gospel. The parallel today would be to use as a model one of the thousands of African refugees risking their lives to cross the Mediterranean to Sicily and Italy in the hope of a better life.

The introduction of an African of course raises the thought as to whether the Magi all came from the same place. Matthew gives us no hint either way, though, probably, the natural way of understanding the text is to think of them travelling together. However, if one, at least, is portrayed as from Asia and another from Africa, the possibility has to be entertained that they travelled from different places, meeting on the way. Whilst this view is entirely speculative, it propels us even more to reflect on the multicultural purpose of Matthew in this chapter. The possibility of the Magi travelling independently, each having set out individually at the provocation of the star required them to meet up on the way. The meeting up in Jerusalem of the Magi, having travelled from different places, in time to meet Herod together, was a popular artistic theme of the 15th century.

The gifts of the Magi of course are at the heart of the painting's narrative. Because of the dense composition of the picture, the gifts, or rather their containers have a striking prominence.

Usually in such pictures the gifts are presented in similar richly decorated caskets. Here the containers themselves are the centre of attention, rather than the gifts they contain, and these illustrate, although in no precise way, the diverse origin of the Magi. The most remarkable of these of course is the Ming porcelain cup, with its lid. This is rarer and possibly more valuable than the gold it contains, and is the most exotic and alien vessel it would have been possible to bring into the picture at that time.

Balthasar presents the frankincense in a rich incense container or holder, very likely based on a Turkish original. Caspar's container for the myrrh is made, most probably, of agate or chalcedony but we know nothing concerning what Mantegna may have used as a model.

In the years before and after Mantegna was working on his masterpiece, Columbus was making his voyages to the New World and new vistas were opening up for all Europeans regarding the meaning of humanity, culture, language , religion and faith. Mantegna's work illustrates the new questions being posed in the late 15th century, and represent a way of addressing them in and through the foundational stories of the Christian Faith. Three Magi, representing three continents, bearing three gifts contained in three vessels of different cultural origin. This really lets the Gospel out of the box!

Offering our very selves

Speculation about the gifts and their meaning can divert us from the very heart of things. We are at the centre of this "gospel in miniature". In the Magi, the nations are being drawn to the vulnerable baby king, who is the God-with-us Saviour, fulfilling ancient biblical promise of God's blessing for all peoples. And in the second phase of the story this Child will begin his ministry in flight as a refugee pursued by the kind of ruthless, blood-stained tyrant with whom the world, ancient and modern, is only too familiar. And in between. . . . *this*. The goal of all this blood, sweat and tears? A needy, broken but dearly loved world bowing before this vulnerable Saviour in worship and in self-offering. He is God's gift to us, and in return we offer the treasure of our own lives to him. "For God so loved the world that he gave his one and only Son . . . ." (John 3:16)

So the first story in Matthew's Gospel calls us to worship as the core meaning of Christian faith, allegiance and discipleship. This worship has two dimensions – we bow, we prostrate ourselves in adoration and awe, and we offer the treasures of our very selves to him. We offer all that we are, and all that we possess. We offer our gifts, the tools of our profession, our aspirations and ambitions. Our lives and our loves.

Mantegna's The Adoration of the Magi , which we reflected on above, rooted as it is in the biblical story, also directs and enriches our understanding of worship. So far we have not thought about the figure of Christ at the centre of the picture and at the centre of devotion . He is the only figure shown full length. As was common among painters of the nativity, the "swaddling bands" in which he is wrapped recall the grave clothes in which he will be wrapped when taken down from the Cross and laid in the tomb. Incarnation and Salvation belong together. The one who is the Word of God, born in Bethlehem is the one who will lay down his life on the Cross, for the whole world – the same world represented by the Magi, just arrived in the Bethlehem home. The Child's right hand is raised in blessing. Or is it simply an instinctive movement by a child? In Mantegna's vision of faith and life the two belong together. Surely, as the Word made flesh, he here blesses the three travellers, whilst his mother offers his foot to us for a kiss.

Dawson Carr in his study of the painting captures well the adoration and awe of the Magi:

> In Mantegna's composition, the Magi are clearly differentiated by states of awe. These faces believe they behold the incarnation of God. At right, Caspar is lost in ecstatic wonder, his mouth agape. Balthasar in the centre is neither fearful or exuberant but mesmerized by the experience. The elderly Melchior presents his gift with his head bowed, not allowing his eyes to meet those of the Child, in a kind of fearful respect that one gives an encounter outside the realm of usual experience, and perhaps reflecting age-old fears of looking directly at God. [xv]

The magnificence of Mantegna's painting is its gracious power in drawing us into the circle of worship. The Magi illustrate the different responses and stances of worship, but we are each drawn in individually. Old Melchior kneels, and the others wait their turn. Our turn will come too.

All our gift-giving at Christmas flows out of this story. As we read it we are most aware of the gifts offered by the Magi. Less visible, but far more profound, is the gift of the Child, the toddler who is at the heart of the story, and the intimate little scene in the house in Bethlehem. God so loved that he gave. . .

May all our gift-giving at Christmas be an act of gratitude for the gift of Christ, and as a small demonstration of the offering of our lives for him and for the Gospel. And may the generosity that flows out of gratitude characterise our living throughout the year.

> What can I give him, poor as I am?
> If I were a shepherd, I would bring a lamb,
> If I were a wise man, I would do my part;
> Yet what I can I give him, give my heart.
>
> Christina Rossetti 1830-94

> Thanks be to God for his indescribable gift!
>
> II Cor. 9:15

C. HOME BY ANOTHER WAY

Angel awakening the Magi; He Qi; www.heqiart.com

And having been warned in a dream not to go back to Herod, they returned to their country by another route. (Matt 2:12)

Another Way

Those magic men, the Magi, some people call them wise or Oriental, even kings.

> Well anyway, those guys, they visited with Jesus, they sure enjoyed their stay.
> Then warned in a dream of King Herod's scheme, they went home by another way
> Yes, they went home by another way, home by another way.
> Maybe me and you can be wise guys too and go home by another way.
> We can make it another way, safe home as they used to say.
> Keep a weather eye to the chart on high and go home another way.

So James Taylor, the great American singer-songwriter! And he's got the point. Matthew concludes the Magi's part in the story in characteristically succinct style. They are warned in a dream – and, sensibly, go home by a different route. We can easily pass on speedily to the next dramatic part of the story. But Matthew signals a further significance through his use of the word "way" (the NIV "route" is accurate enough, but not helpful here). We are aware that Christians at first were called followers of the "The Way" (Acts 22:4). Interestingly it was in Antioch – possibly, as we have seen, Matthew's home city - that the transition was made from being called "followers of the Way" to "Christians" (Acts 11: 26)

The description of following Christ as being a "Way" is important to Matthew. Jesus says:

> Enter by the narrow gate; for the gate is wide and the way is easy that leads to destruction, and those who enter it are many.

For the gate is narrow and the way is hard that leads to life and those who find it are few.

(Matthew 7:13, Revised Standard Version)

Being on the narrow and hard way is decisive for a person's journey to "life". There is a strong likelihood that Matthew is signalling a spiritual as well as a physical change of direction in this verse in chapter 2. The Magi had arrived by the broad and easy but the destructive way that had brought them past Herod. Now, having worshipped at the feet of the true King of the Jews, and warned in a dream, they returned home by a far narrower and more difficult way. Geographically, to avoid Herod's territory and spies, it may well have taken them via Gaza to Egypt and on to Arabia. Spiritually, in the light of their significant journey as the first representatives of the nations coming to the light and the blessing of the Messiah, they return changed, new men, travelling a different way.

The passage has been read this way from early times[xvi]. Matthew gives us no hint or speculation as to what was their route home, what was the reception that awaited them, or what ongoing impact the experience of their journey had upon them. It has fallen to later poets and writers to hazard a guess at that.

James Taylor doesn't get much further than warning against being haunted for the rest of your life by the memory of Herod, and the world's cruelty:

Home is where they want you now,
you can more or less assume that you'll be welcome in the end.

Mustn't let King Herod haunt you so or fantasize when you're looking at a friend. . .
But Herod's always out there, he's got our cards on file.
It's a lead pipe cinch, if we give an inch, and Herod likes to take a mile.
It's best to go home by another way, home by another way.

For T. S. Eliot's Magi too, the return was ambiguous and full of uncertainties. But the questionings of the elderly Magus of the poem, many years later, searches out the meaning of the story more profoundly:

All this was a long time ago, I remember,
And I would do it again, but set down
This set down
This: were we led all that way for
Birth or Death? There was a Birth, certainly,
We had evidence and no doubt. I had seen birth and death,
But thought they were different; this Birth was
Hard and bitter agony for us, like Death, our death.
We returned to our palaces, these Kingdoms,
But no longer at ease here, in the old dispensation,
With an alien people clutching their gods,
I should be glad of another death.

The elderly Magus is aware that there had been more to the Bethlehem encounter with the Child than met the eye. Only vaguely grasped by the visitors, this Birth had within it the seeds of a Death, it was a Birth for the Cross, hinted at earlier in the poem by the reference to "three trees on the low sky". So strangely the experience was not unalloyed joy, but "hard and bitter agony for us". As the elderly Simeon had warned Mary in the Temple when she and Joseph took Jesus to be presented, "A sword will pierce your own soul too." And even so, this Magus, grief and joy, hardship and ease, life and death, "would do it all again"!

Eliot explores also in imagination how the Magus felt in his home country. Despite the hardships of the journey and the painful ambiguities of the encounter, the Magi have been irrevocably changed. They are "no longer at ease" in the society where they had once been respected religious and spiritual experts. Somehow, we are not told how, they know themselves to be in a new dispensation, a new phase of world history, shaped by the Child of Bethlehem which rendered the values and perceptions of the surrounding society obsolete. "The old dispensation, with an alien people clutching their gods" no longer holds them.

He can now face his own mortality: "I should be glad of another death."

Our own way home

Matthew invites us to make the Magi's story our story too. The place where the deep desire of nations and people is fulfilled is in the human reality of Jesus. The divine homecoming for which we seek is hidden within this one human life. We may find him first in the vulnerable child of a simple home in Bethlehem; or in the preacher and teacher of Galilee, the broken body of the man on the Cross, or encounter him as the one risen and victorious over death. One encounter will lead us on to the others for in this man the wisdom, grace and truth of God are incarnate.

The questions that follow are straightforward, though their answering will take a lifetime. What do you offer him? How will you be changed? What is your new Way home? And what will the "homecoming" be like? Will you, in the words T S Eliot gives to his Magus, be "no longer at ease in the old dispensation"? Or perhaps, quoting other well-known words of Eliot:

> With the drawing of this Love and the voice of this calling
>
> We shall not cease from exploration
> And the end of all our exploring
> Will be to arrive where we started
> And know the place for the first time.

PART 3: THE JOURNEY OF THE CHILD.

Out of Egypt have I called my son; Magdy William; Author's Picture

Flight from Egypt; He Qi; www.heqiart.com

CHAPTER 7.

FLIGHT

Matthew, chapter 2:

> **13** When they had gone, an angel of the Lord appeared to Joseph in a dream. "Get up," he said, "take the child and his mother and escape to Egypt. Stay there until I tell you, for Herod is going to search for the child to kill him."
>
> **14** So he got up, took the child and his mother during the night and left for Egypt, **15** where he stayed until the death of Herod. And so was fulfilled what the Lord had said through the prophet, "Out of Egypt have I called my son."

World in Flight

We Refugees

By the first dream,
 I was assured:
Mary was faithful,
 Not fooling around.
That was fulfilled.

By the second dream,
 I was warned:
We three refugees
 Needed to flee.
This was frightening.

Watching the news in the summer and autumn of 2013 and on into 2014 was a searing and brutal experience.

Serried rows of tents stretched to the horizon: dust, aid workers' Landcruisers, clusters of children inventing games to play, stressed faces of adults framed by canvas. An estimated 9 million Syrians had left their homes in the years since 2011, 3 million of them fleeing to neighbouring countries. Turkey, Lebanon,

We took the road South,
To Gentile territory,
Terrified.
Oppressive or safe?
Who could tell?

Sad and miserable,
Sleepless nights,
Hungry and thirsty,
On the move,
Hardships, distress.

How can we sing
The Lord's song
In a strange land?
How long, O Lord?

Owning nothing,
Yet, with this child,
Possessing everything.

Jordan and Iraq were overwhelmed. Turkey had received a million refugees. Well over a million Syrian children were refugees outside their own country. It was the biggest refugee and humanitarian crisis of modern times[xvii].

Extraordinary levels of brutality and destruction had become the norm over a couple of years: small arms everywhere, aerial bombings, houses reduced to rubble. In a further shocking twist, extraordinary savagery on the part of the so-called Islamic State - massacres, beheadings, and crucifixions - had caused many communities in Iraq to flee in blind terror. Christian communities and distinctive religious and cultural communities like the Yazidis fled their ancient homelands. Aid workers were beheaded, recorded on video and the execution displayed on the internet.

Ukraine, South Sudan, Libya. . . I have sat in helpless anguish, as, doubtless, we all have. We live in an age of migration, of displacement. By mid 2015 it was said that half a million African people were camped in Libya waiting for their opportunity to risk their lives to cross the Mediterranean Sea in search of a better life in Europe. Thousands have perished at sea as traffickers have abandoned them at the first sign of trouble. Naval ships of several nationalities attempt to rescue hundreds from the water. At the eastern fringes of the Mediterranean thousands of refugees from terror and violence in Syria, Iraq and Afghanistan find ways of crossing to the Greek Islands, themselves facing economic meltdown.

Our world is a world in which millions are in transit, running in fear, insecurity, poverty as well as in hope, seeking a new home, a new life, where they will find safety, freedom from fear, education, work and a better future for their children. Nearer home, for British people that is, thousands from all corners of the world crowd into Calais, willing to risk their lives to seize a momentary opportunity to escape to Britain on a truck.

In the same few weeks we also had thrust into our awareness the grief and pain of thousands of children in our own country, trafficked, abused, betrayed. A published report concerned Rotherham, but similar stories can be found across the country. Tear Fund have just launched a long-term programme and appeal called "No Child Taken." They report that across the world "3000 children a day – more than one million children a year" are trafficked into various forms of slavery, sexual exploitation, conscription as child soldiers, and abuse.

The news over these months has simply brought before us in ways we cannot ignore or escape the ongoing realities of our world. Insecurity, fear, desperation, destitution and flight are everyday realities for millions. It seemed as if, very abruptly, a safety net against inhumanity and savagery had been taken away. Never before, for me at least, had the Biblical understanding of all human beings as made in God's image seemed so precious, so desperately needed and so under threat.

The King's Flight

Do our Christmas stories address this? Do they help us understand and give us tools for living positively and usefully in such a world? We invariably conclude our Christmas reading in Matthew's Gospel at chapter 2, verse 12. The Magi open their gifts before the Christ Child, are then warned in a dream, and return home avoiding Herod. Here ends the reading, and here ends the story.

Matthew's story is, however, richer and deeper than this truncated version allows. We are only half way.

Matthew's story has this basic structure:

THE JOURNEY TO THE KING - Matt 2:1-8 →
WORSHIPPING THE KING - Matt 2: 9-12 →
THE JOURNEY OF THE KING - Matt 2: 13-23

The Magi, in their star-led pilgrimage, persevere past the perils of Herod, to the feet of the Child. Gathered there, they represent the eventual goal of God's mission into the world. Promised to Abraham, the blessing of the nations is beginning in the only place it can – in the presence of the Son of Abraham, the Son of David, Jesus, the Saviour of the world, Emmanuel. Here they have offered their treasures – symbols of their trade, symbols of the saving ministry of the Messiah. The healing of the nations has begun. Its fulfilment will be described in John's Revelation:

> "Now the dwelling place of God is with men, and he will live with them. They will be his people, and God himself will be with them and be their God. He will wipe away every tear from their eyes."
>
> The kings of the earth will bring their splendour into the city (the new Jerusalem) . . . The glory and honour of the nations will be brought into it.
>
> (Revelation 21:3-4. 24-26)

So what happens now, now that the exotic eastern guests have departed? The Mission of the Messiah begins! With no delay we are plunged straight into what it means for the God-with-us Saviour to embark on his mission into a dark and alienated world.

The story that Matthew now unfolds is extraordinary. These are doubtless the narrative elements he inherited, but it is risky story telling indeed. As an initial presentation of the gospel message, this could be seriously misunderstood. As we shall see, it is fundamental "gospel teaching", but it is wholly contrary to what his readers might expect. We do not see the life-giving powers of the King being instantly demonstrated. Rather it is the death-obsessed forces of evil that are unleashed. A deadly battle has commenced.

Joseph was warned in a dream that Herod's bloodthirsty paranoia has been aroused by the failure of his Magi spies. In the middle of the night, Joseph wakened Mary and, sweeping the Child into his arms, and gathering a few belongings, fled southwards in the darkness with his wife. Their route probably took them first past Hebron, and then through Gaza (ironically a refugee settlement of the 20th and 21st centuries), and down the so-called Desert Road to Egypt[xviii]. It is about 150 miles, and more than a week of travelling. Both Gaza and Egypt are well acquainted with refugees.

This is stunning. In this "gospel in miniature", as the story of salvation begins, there are no fanfares, no trumpets, no demonstrations of power, no adoring crowds – but a vulnerable family with a toddler fleeing for their lives to a foreign country. Emmanuel is *here,* this is how God is "with us". How many times have we seen such scenes on our television screens in recent times?

This Child, helpless now, will not be so vulnerable and helpless again until he is the Man on the Cross. He is silent now, he will be silent then.

> "He saved others, but he cannot save himself!"
> (Matthew 27:42)

The shadow of the Cross falls across this passage. Commonly when Renaissance artists painted nativity scenes, the "swaddling clothes" of the baby appear like grave clothes, reminding us of the destiny of the child in the manger. In Andrea Mantegna's Adoration of the Magi which we considered in Ch.6, the Christ Child's clothes resemble grave clothes, but he wears them rather like a Roman toga, illustrating the authority of both the incarnate one and the crucified one. It is a lovely and moving touch.

This is indeed risky story telling – but its resonance with the modern world is strong. We are in the midst of an extended commemoration of the First World War. We know how it ushered in a terrible century of war, violence and hatred. Edward Shillitoe's poem "Jesus of the Scars", published in the wake of the First World War, finds the words for many:

> If we have never sought, we seek Thee now;
> Thine eyes burn through the dark, our only stars;
> We must have sight of thorn-pricks on Thy brow;
> We must have Thee, O Jesus of the Scars. . .
>
> The other gods were strong, but Thou wast weak
> They rode, but Thou didst stumble to a throne;
> But to our wounds only God's wounds speak;
> And not a god has wounds, but Thou alone.[xix]

The Second World War only deepened the relevance of this unsettling but fundamental feature of the Gospel – the vulnerability and weakness of God as made evident in the whole event of Jesus' life, ministry, death and resurrection. Jorgen Moltmann's book The Crucified God arose out of his experience of the Second World War and his experience as a prisoner of war. The title has captured an essential insight for our age, even for many who have never read his book.

However, this vulnerability, this weakness is not just somehow a demonstration of the defeat of God, or the uselessness of faith in the face of ruthless power. It is the beginning of a revolution. A revolution that is rooted in God's full taking of our humanity upon himself, fully owning it, as it were. *Totus in nobis* – totally one of us – as Pope Leo the Great put it.

This is what it means to take on humanity. This is no pretence, no play-acting. The God-with-us Saviour truly shares our human experience, and so truly flees for his life, becoming a refugee, knowing fear, hunger and insecurity. Once during our years in South Sudan living through the civil war, we had to flee from advancing rebel troops. With 24 hours notice, we gathered passports and precious possessions and fled in a Landcruiser, rather than on a donkey, down the 200 miles from Mundri to Yei. Our daughter Clare was a toddler of about two years. Arriving in Yei, we were kindly given a small house to stay in. All had gone well. But Clare, hardly understanding what was happening, was only aware of being in a strange bed, in a strange house, after a long gruelling day, with anxious and disorientated parents. She wept inconsolably that night.

Such was the experience of the Son of God on the road south to Egypt. This true and vulnerable humanity is what he bears to the Cross, carrying its guilt and sorrow. And this is the humanity, healed and restored in the resurrection, into which we are born again.

Could it be any other way?

> Yet with all the risks, its agonies and tragedies, there is no other conceivable environment (i.e. this world) in which responsive self-giving love, to say nothing of courage, compassion or self-sacrifice, could have evolved. To speak in crudely human terms, the choice before God has been this or nothing. And, in a sense, that is the ultimate choice each one of us has to come to, for, as I have already said, "I believe in God" is a vote of confidence in the Creator and in the blood-stained enterprise in which willy-nilly he has involved us and himself.[xx]

John Taylor's shocking phrase jolts us out of our complacency and compels us to face again the pain of our world and the challenges of believing in a loving God in the midst of it. Authentic Christian discipleship seeks to hold both together at the same time, insisting that it is indeed in just such a world that we need to find and live out the love of God.

Jesus' words need to be appropriated again and again, "If anyone would come after me, he must deny himself and take up his cross and follow me." (Mark 8:34) When Jesus commissions Peter at a resurrection breakfast to "Feed my sheep" (John 21: 15ff) the calling comes with an assurance of the price involved:

> Jesus said, "I tell you the truth, when you were younger you dressed yourself and went where you wanted: but when you are old you will stretch out your hands, and someone else will dress you and lead where you do not want to go." Jesus said this to indicate the kind of death by which Peter would glorify God.

According to tradition, Peter was executed by Emperor Nero by crucifixion like his Lord. Luther's insistence that true Christian theology is a "theologia crucis" – a theology of the cross – rather than any kind of "theologia gloriae," is salutary and an anchor here.

This does not simplify Christian discipleship. Rather it complicates it and adds levels of ambiguity. In a dangerous world, where religion and culture are inflamed by history, and where social exclusion and hopelessness engender violence and nihilism, how can the Christian responsibly exercise leadership and power? How does the Christian play his part in the exercise of military and political responsibility? How can "self-giving love", in Taylor's phrase, in the complex and emotionally over-heated public debate of today, be demonstrated, be proclaimed and change the human heart? What we know from Matthew's courageous presentation is that the God-with-us Saviour is nonetheless present in fearful, enclosed Bethlehem, on the Gaza road, in the ruthless political circles of Jerusalem, with the refugees flooding into Cairo, with the prisoner, with the lonely and desperate, then and now. It is God, this God, or nothing.

Flight into Egypt

Flight into Egypt is a common motif in the Bible. It is a place of refuge, and a place of temptation. For Abraham it was both. He took refuge there at a time of famine (Gen. 12:13). But aware of Sarah's beauty and anxious for his personal safety, he passed her off as his sister, an act of deceit that only led to deeper problems when the Pharaoh of the day wanted her as his wife (for which, see the rest of Gen. 12!). Later Joseph was sold as a slave by his brothers to traders who sold him on to a royal official in Egypt, where he was used to save his family from destitution when they later came to Egypt at a time of famine (Gen. 37-50). What had initially been a land of refuge became a place of slavery from which God, through the leadership of Moses, eventually delivered his people.

Later again Jeremiah was taken to Egypt against his will by the remaining Jewish leadership in Jerusalem when Judah and its capital city were under overwhelming threat from the Babylonian Nebuchadnezzar (Jer. 41-43, II Kings 25: 25-26).

Jeremiah is reputed to have died there. Scattered by the various disasters that overwhelmed Judah and Jerusalem then and in subsequent years, a very large community of Jews grew up in Egypt. Alexandria by the 1st century reputedly had as many as a million Jewish inhabitants, constituting a third of the population[xxi]. This community was predominantly Greek-speaking, and produced a number of distinguished religious leaders and philosophers. Most notable amongst these was Philo, an almost exact contemporary of Jesus, chiefly remembered for his attempts to synthesize Jewish religious principles and Greek rationalism and philosophy. Later Christian thinkers, attempting a similar task in Christian theology, saw him as a forerunner of Christianity.

It was here in Alexandria that the Septuagint, the influential Greek translation of the Hebrew scriptures, was prepared. This version of the Old Testament scriptures was the usual text available to the writers of the New Testament. There were even two Jewish temples in Egypt (alternatives to the Jerusalem Temple) that offered animal sacrifices on the Jerusalem pattern at least in certain periods. The more renowned of these was at Elephantine in Aswan.

Egypt was well-known as home to all manner of magical and occultist practices. So the Christian tradition of Jesus' early childhood being spent in Egypt appears to have provided the grounds for hostile rabbinic allegations, dating from as early as the end of the 1st century, that Egypt was where Jesus learned the magic arts that enabled him to "lead Israel astray."[xxii] These allegations probably arise from some awareness of Matthew's narrative, rather than constituting independent evidence for the family's stay in Egypt.

So in fleeing to Egypt, Joseph and Mary would have known that substantial Jewish communities awaited them there. Matthew gives us no detail concerning where they stayed; only that they stayed until after the death of Herod in 4BC. If Jesus was born in 7BC, the Family may have stayed in Egypt for as long as four or five years. In compensation, the Coptic Orthodox Church has very extensive traditions concerning the stay of the Holy Family. Interestingly the main traditions do not include Alexandria in the itinerary, which otherwise takes in all the major Christian and monastic centres of Christianity throughout Egypt as far south as modern day Assiut. For the Egyptian Church of all branches the story of the Holy Family in Egypt and its associated traditions is of the highest importance. Generally in the Bible Egypt has a rather negative image. But outweighing them far is the fact that it was in Egypt that the Holy Family found safety and refuge and that it was from Egypt that the Family returned to Israel, to the Holy Land. The foundation text for the Egyptian Church, quoted frequently by Coptic Christians, might well be:

> Out of Egypt have I called my son.
> (Hosea 11:1 & Matt 2: 15)

To this text can be added Isaiah 19, a text from the Old Testament that has rooted the Egyptian Church in their sense of having a place in God's purpose and blessing, especially its final verse:

> The Lord Almighty will bless them, saying, "Blessed be Egypt my people."

Refuge Egypt

In 1990 Cairo was awash with African refugees. Eritreans and Ethiopians were fleeing the bitter conflict that would result in Eritrean independence. Northern Sudanese were fleeing the brutality of an Islamist military regime in Khartoum, and Southern Sudanese were fleeing the combined miseries of flooding, famine and government-sponsored ethnic cleansing by Arab Baggara militia. In addition there were Nigerians escaping a corrupt military government and economic meltdown, and smaller numbers from Congo/Zaire, Zimbabwe, Libya and elsewhere. Many were Christians and so found their way to the churches of Cairo and Alexandria.

St Andrew's Church in the heart of the city, Scottish Presbyterian by origin, had risen to the challenge and in its refugee programme provided financial and practical assistance, educational and training programmes. Additionally the Catholic Church in Abbasiya, across the city had a vigorous programme for Sudanese refugees. With a beautiful symmetry this very church had been the Cairo centre for Daniel Comboni, 19th century pioneer missionary to Sudan, and his confreres. Fr. Cosimo Spadevecchia, a Comboni Missionary himself, ran a school, social activities and a weekly Mass for Sudanese refugees.

However, many of the growing number of refugees from South Sudan thronged to All Saints Cathedral, on Zamalek island in the middle of the Nile. Many of them were Anglicans, so felt at home here. Additionally, for historical reasons (Egypt's long-standing claim to sovereignty in the Nile Valley) they had the right of abode in Egypt, though no right to work. As a result they were "displaced" rather than refugees, didn't qualify for assistance from the UN High Commission for Refugees, and were trapped in desperate poverty.

We arrived in Cairo as a young family with two small children just before Christmas in 1989. Our agenda was to stay, perhaps for about 6 months, to improve our limited Arabic and then move to Khartoum to work with the Episcopal Church of the Sudan. Visa problems and a deteriorating political situation in Sudan, meant that we stayed about two and a half years. But even in Cairo we rapidly became immersed in Sudan's burgeoning misery. We lived in a 5th floor flat overlooking the cathedral from where we could see the daily tide of refugees from South Sudan, negotiating their way past the government security guards, seeking a temporary refuge from harassment and intimidation on the streets. They came for a place of quiet, a place of prayer, a mug of tea, and what little assistance might be available.

A small "Sudanese Programme" had been running for a couple of years, supporting a small number in the production of sisal baskets and other crafts to sell in the expatriate community. This endeavour was being overwhelmed by the new arrivals from the south. Thousands were on the move. Fleeing the widespread violence and brutality in the war-torn South, they made their way to Khartoum in the hope of safety, education and employment. There they found only further abuse, threats and grinding poverty. They continued down the Nile, by bus, by foot, and by ferry. Reaching Wadi Halfa, they argued, bribed or somehow scrambled their way across the frontier into Egypt, continuing in desperation, exhaustion and hunger across the desert down the several hundred miles to Cairo where, they trusted, all would be well. This is where we met them – huddling in the cathedral compound or on the streets, shivering with cold (it was winter), hungry and fearful. Sue and I picked up the fragile Sudanese Programme and tried to offer some small measure of support. One winter evening Sue went down to the street markets in Atbara and bought 50 sweaters for new arrivals clad in little more than a T-shirt.

Once again Egypt had become, through the ministry of the churches, a refuge for those fleeing violence and oppression.[xxiii] In a basement below the cathedral offices a small ministry began to unfold. Sue started a programme to welcome and listen to all new arrivals. Many she met herself. Trained Sudanese colleagues also helped. Each new arrival, as far as we could manage, found a listening ear and an opportunity to tell their story. Mostly it was young men who found their way to Cairo – but there were also families, or mothers on their own struggling to care for children. The modest help we were able to provide included linking up new arrivals with others in Cairo from their home area who might be able to care a little for them. There were also small, very small, gifts of money, clothes and food. Gradually social life began to build. A tea shop, mostly for refugees was established in the compound: also a medical programme, mainly for families and expectant mothers, new income-generating craft activities, a weekly Bible study, and Sunday worship in a diversity of local Sudanese languages (Dinka, Moru, and Bari especially).

And: a Sunday lunch. Mostly the Sudanese were living in very crowded flats in desperately poor areas of the city, sharing beds, sleeping on the floor. What they lacked were places to relax, to talk, to meet friends. And they certainly lacked a good solid meal. Little knowing how it would develop, we opened our home to the community. Some young women, on their own in the city, came to live with us (and baby-sit the children). Others came in and out through the week for a chat, some space, a small sense of family. But on Sunday all were invited to lunch in our flat which was fortunately quite spacious. It began with a dozen or so, but gradually grew until it was 60 or 80 or even more. A couple from the British Embassy, Alan and Lillian, provided two big trays of food every week – cottage pie, roast chicken pieces stand out in the memory. We provided some bread and a little salad. Strangely, no matter how the numbers grew, there was always enough food. Everyone had a full plate. We sat on the chairs, on the floor, in the lounge, down the hallway. And we sang. Someone had a guitar, and our sense of being Sudanese, of being Christian, of being both a refugee and a pilgrim people was nourished as we sang Juba Arabic songs, popular Christian songs in English, and some stomping songs that we shouted at the top of our voices like "We are Marching in the Light of God" from South Africa.

As for the Holy Family, so for this vulnerable, rootless community, Egypt had become a place of safety, a place where a sense of being family could be recovered, where hopefulness for the future could be nurtured. And down in the cathedral compound stood a stone monument, rescued from the original Anglican Cathedral beside the Nile that had been demolished years before, proclaiming "Out of Egypt have I called my Son!"

And so almost all that community of pilgrims have moved on, "out of Egypt." They are, perhaps, aware of being "called out", or perhaps just aware of being swept along by the irresistible drives of the search for education, safety and self-preservation. Many have returned to the newly independent country of South

Sudan. Others have found new lives in the USA, Canada or Australia. Many found a new confidence, a new faith, and new tools for making their way in a ruthless and unheeding world.

And we too were "called out" – on, as it turned out, to Nairobi to work with the New Sudan Council of Churches and closer to the civil war in South Sudan and the suffering, death and desolation it was wreaking.

But Egypt's role as a welcomer of the refugee and the stranger continues. Refugees flee to Egypt, still from Sudan, but also from a host of other African and Middle Eastern countries. Our quite modest "Sudanese Programme" has become a much larger, comprehensive and effective ministry, still based in the cathedral basement, called "Refuge Egypt" . Most recently hundreds of refugees from Syria have found their way to Cairo, and to the cathedral where the UNHCR registers them, but where a team of Christians provide tea and something to eat, and play with the children.

Moses and Israel: Matthew's framework

At first sight it may seem that Egypt itself has little significance for Matthew. The story is told simply, efficiently and without elaboration. But this phase of the story has rich resonance for him.

There is a *geographical* significance to the flight into Egypt. This is not merely some logistical inconvenience, like being re-routed on an air journey. Israel had spent much of its history juggling relations with the East (Assyria, Babylon, Persia), and with the South (Egypt). She had been in slavery in Egypt, and in exile in

Babylon. Both experiences had combined desolation and despair with new beginnings, new encounter with God and with deliverance. Both regions had been consistent military and political threats to Israel and later the southern kingdom of Judah. The Israelite kingdoms were continually being seduced by the power and the gods of the great empires to east and to south.

Now, with this dramatic, yet subtle and elusive, new initiative of the God of Israel, something was afoot to transform these dependent, oppressive yet alluring relationships. In the pilgrims from the East with which Matthew's story begins, those ancient enemies were coming at last in fulfilment of the scriptural promises to the feet of Israel's God. And now, even that most ancient of foes, Egypt, was being brought positively and creatively into the story of salvation. For it was out of Egypt, now a place of safety not of slavery, that God would bring his son, back to his homeland and the scene of the drama of human redemption.

For Matthew the fact that the Holy Family fled to Egypt has two main biblical and theological resonances. Both are clearly present although they pull in rather different directions. First, Matthew clearly sees in Jesus' story a parallel with that of Moses. Jesus is the new Moses, a theme which will surface repeatedly later in the Gospel. Both as young baby boys are threatened by the intentions of a tyrant king to kill Jewish boys, albeit in different countries – Jesus by Herod in Judea, Moses by Pharaoh in Egypt. They both escape, Moses as an adult, and take refuge, one in Egypt, the other in Sinai. And both later are able to return now that "those who seek your life are dead" (Ex. 4:19 & Matt 2:20). And both are the Deliverers, the Saviours of their people, leading them out of bondage into freedom and a promised land.

The other biblical resonance for Matthew identifies Jesus as the "new Israel", the new "Son of God" bearing God's purpose. This enables Matthew to include the Hosea quotation to which I have already referred: "Out of Egypt have I called my son" (Hos. 11:1). Just as "Israel" in the shape of Jacob (whose other name is, after all, Israel) with his extended family, went down to Egypt to escape famine, so Jesus now escapes to Egypt. The context of the Hosea passage concerns Israel's unfaithfulness and deficiencies as God's son. Notwithstanding, in the Exodus God brought his son out of Egypt to accomplish his purpose in the Land he had promised. And Jesus, who by contrast will perfectly fulfil his Father's will, now worthily fulfils this word from the Old Testament. God will indeed bring his Son out of Egypt.[xxiv]

Matthew's narrative is spare and direct, but still bears a rich biblical hinterland. The great salvation themes and figures of the Old Testament are woven into this narrative of Jesus' early years to alert us to the immense significance of the wider story of Jesus ministry, death and resurrection. "Jesus is New Israel in person, the fulfilled promise wrapped in the life of a single Jewish child" [xxv].This is the one for whom all history has been waiting.

Travels in Egypt

Matthew tells us nothing of the years that the Holy Family spent in Egypt. They are as "hidden" as the years in Nazareth. For the Church in Egypt, however, the fact that Egypt was a place of refuge for the Son of God, and that it was from this land that God called his Son has provoked imagination, reflection and interpretation. In Coptic tradition, much of it very ancient, the Holy Family traversed much of Egypt as far as Assiut to the north of Luxor. Monasteries and churches mark the places they rested, resided for a time, confronted pagan and demonic forces, worked miracles or embarked for travels up the Nile. Whatever credence we may give to these stories, and for Copts they are a deeply rooted part of their history and Christian understanding, they do serve several important purposes in the self-understanding of the Christian community.

These stories give flesh and a narrative to the redemption of Egypt's Bible story – for it is out of *Egypt* (of all places!) that God called his Son. And in his Egyptian sojourn the Son of God and his parents visited and by their presence consecrated many of the places which later became monastic and church centres. Thus many of the Christian centres in Egypt have a quite special sanctity, given by the visit of Christ in the flesh. Egypt thus becomes a second "Holy Land". During the many centuries in which the Church has lived under Muslim rule[xxvi], with constant pressure on its life and with occasional outright persecution, these stories have given assurance of God's presence in their country, together with the special history and blessings in which it partakes. Egypt is a land of miracles as is the Holy Land itself. Amongst the more extraordinary features of these stories, is the occasional encounter with people that we more normally associate with the Gospel stories. For example, during their travels up the Nile, the Holy Family is described in some traditions as encountering Lazarus (whom Jesus later raised from death[xxvii]). They are also pursued and harassed by the two thieves with whom Jesus will eventually be crucified. The Bethlehem shepherds seek them out – and they are pursued up the Nile by Herod's soldiers, frustrated in their search for Herod's rival as King of the Jews.[xxviii] These stories seem, to western eyes, to be particularly fanciful. What are they about?

These stories both give further context to the accounts in the Gospels and establish Egypt as another Holy Land, or perhaps as part of the one Holy Land. Thus, we understand why Jesus was particularly at home in the home of Mary, Martha and Lazarus – he and Lazarus had met before. And the conversation on the cross between Jesus and the two thieves gains even greater poignancy when we realise that long before in Egypt the Holy Family had suffered at their hands[xxix].

The first part of Matthew's chapter portrayed a narrowing, a focusing, as the journey of the Magi gradually centred on Bethlehem and the family dwelling there with their immense secret. But the second part of the chapter portrays a widening out. The adoration of the Christ Child by the Magi lets loose the secret of the Gospel, the subversive, bottom-side up revolution that the living God is initiating in a world consumed by self-seeking power and violence. From this point the story widens. The closing verses of the Gospel will record the Lord sending out his disciples to "make disciples of all nations, baptising them. . . and teaching them. . . And surely I am with you always, to the very end of the age."[xxx]

How far shall we travel? For now, with Matthew, we go as far as Egypt, with its hints of the battles that lie ahead for a message centred on the vulnerable Child of Bethlehem. Alexandria where Pharaonic, Greek and Jewish wisdom existed uncomfortably side by side; hungry, disease-ridden communities up and down the Nile longing for a divine intervention; temples with their priests and vested interests whose idols, the traditions tell us, fell at the feet of the Child. The Holy Family may be in head-long flight from Herod's soldiers, but that flight takes them into the complex, multi-layered worlds where the Gospel will have to make its way.

Massacre of the Innocents; Lucas Cranach, the Elder;
National Museum of Warsaw

CHAPTER 8.

BITTER COST

Matthew, chapter 2:

> **16** When Herod realised that he had been outwitted by the Magi, he was furious, and he gave orders to kill all the boys in Bethlehem and its vicinity who were two years old and under, in accordance with the time he had learned from the Magi. **17**
> Then what was said by the prophet Jeremiah was fulfilled:
>
> **18** 'A voice was heard in Ramah,
> weeping and great mourning,
> Rachel weeping for her children
> and refusing to be comforted,
> because they are no more.'"

Terror Unleashed

Outwitted, outmanoeuvred,
Herod unleashes terror.

Revenge, outraged, ventures out,
Unresisted, unrestrained.

Many are slaughtered to slay the One:
The One survives to save the many.

Hurting Children

Frederick Dale Bruner in his massive commentary on Matthew makes the following comment on this passage, "Those who begin by hating the Child end by hurting children[xxxi]." It is a pungent and painful observation. Is it really true that the violent rejection of Christ has such dehumanising results?

I think of the chilling film footage of Hitler in the last days of the Third Reich playfully pinching the faces of a row of young boys as he awards them medals and sends them out to die against the overwhelming forces of the Soviet Union. Or of more recent accounts and photographs of the soldiers of the Islamic State in Iraq brutally and casually butchering small children, many of them from Christian families, others from other religious and ethnic groups.

Nearer to home, yesterday, as I was thinking ahead to the writing of this chapter, two news items appeared on the television. The first concerned the annual fundraising festival of the BBC called "Children in Need" which raises huge amounts of money (this year £32m) to support children's charities in the UK. But the other concerned the wrenching news that the ongoing enquiry into the alleged sexual and physical abuse of large numbers of children in the 70s and 80s by senior establishment figures in the military, the media, the law, the Church, politics and high society, had taken a further twist with the possibility of murder and manslaughter charges. Slaughter of the Innocents indeed.

Once we have begun such a reflection on the vulnerability and suffering of children in our world, the stories begin to flow. In 1989, government-funded Arabic militias from Northern Sudan raided border areas in South Sudan, raiding, burning, looting and enslaving those they found. Western Bahr el Ghazal was devastated, becoming a desert for years to come. Many of the women and girls were taken off northwards to become domestic slaves in the cities of Northern Sudan, or forced labour on the plantations and farms. The southern rebel forces known as the SPLA (Sudan People's Liberation Army) gathered up tens of thousands of young boys, mostly between the ages of six and about twelve, and marched them off 600 miles eastwards to the refugee and military training camps in Ethiopia. They were destined to become a "Jesh Amar", a young radical "Red Army" for the SPLA. They tramped across waterless wastes as well as crossing the swamps and waterways of the Nile. Food was scarce, mercy unobtainable. Thousands died along the way of thirst, hunger, disease and sheer exhaustion. Asked how they found their way, one small boy replied, "We followed the bones"[xxxii]. By God's grace, as they arrived, gaunt, traumatised and sick, they fell into the arms of the Anglican Church's Mothers Union. Through the churches, their training as young shock troops was tempered by church primary school lessons and church choir rehearsals. Many died, many never recovered; others became dedicated soldiers, others became the advance "troops" of an evangelistic revival across Southern Sudan.

Whether it is modern sex trafficking of young girls, abuse in its many forms, the protection of the powerful and privileged, "Hating Christ" and "Hurting children" continue to be themes in close association in our own times. Bruner continues, "Hating revelation leads to hurting people. If people will be ungodly they will be inhumane. Herod is the Gospel's earliest evidence of this[xxxiii] ". We should note too that, throughout this passage, Jesus is known only as "the Child". He is one with, he stands for, and represents, all those slain in Bethlehem, and all those abused and mistreated since. He is "a child." He is "The Child." And does the knowledge of this childhood event in any way lie behind Jesus' unusual and culturally ground-breaking awareness of the significance of children to God, and in the Kingdom?

> He called a little child and had him stand among them. And he said, "I tell you the truth, unless you change and become like little children, you will never enter the kingdom of heaven. Therefore, whoever humbles himself like this child is the greatest in the kingdom of heaven.
>
> And whoever welcomes a little child like this in my name welcomes me. But if anyone causes one of these little ones who believe in me to sin, it would be better for him to have a large millstone hung around his neck and be drowned in the depths of the sea.
>
> (Matthew 18:2-6)

It is The Child speaking.

Unspeakable Brutality

But let us return to Matthew's story-telling. Having taken us in imagination with the Holy Family in flight to Egypt, we now learn the cause, the desperate necessity for that flight. The deception of the Magi triggered Herod's murderous fear and anger. He sent troops to Bethlehem and in an attempt to sweep the new born baby king into oblivion, gave order that they slaughter all baby boys under the age of two years – following the timing given to him by the Magi.

At this point all romance, all "prettiness" in the story vanishes. This is no longer a story for the children, a Christmas entertainment. This pitches us straight into the kind of brutal, mindless, merciless killing that scars and traumatises many communities in our age, as in any other. Bethlehem in the time of Herod is Syria, Mosul, Gaza, South Sudan. It is the Somme, Passchendaele, Stalingrad, Auschwitz and Hiroshima. It is the genocides of Armenia, Rwanda and Cambodia.

You must know, says Matthew, that the coming of the Messiah, the Son of David, the Son of Abraham into this world, is an immersion into its most painful realities. It addresses and confronts human cruelty and inhumanity at its very worst. More than that, you must know, he says, that his coming into the world provokes the forces of hatred and violence to resist and eliminate him. Every Herod, every evil stronghold, will be out for his blood. There will be collateral damage in this redemptive struggle.

As with the story of the flight into Egypt. Matthew is taking great risks with his story-telling. Immanuel – the God who is with us – is powerless to prevent the Bethlehem bloodbath. As Bethlehem's mothers shriek to the heavens, the heavens offer no comfort. Immanuel himself is fleeing down the road to Egypt.

Kenneth Bailey, many years a New Testament scholar in the Middle East, asks "Why did Matthew think it important to record this unspeakably brutal act?" And he answers, "Was it because love had an inexpressible incarnation at the same time and in the same place?"[xxxiv] There it is. We are invited to draw near, to stand and see – the unbearable reality of human sin, pride and rebellion against God, and the unimaginable beauty and costliness of the love that came to dwell with us in Bethlehem. This is the desperately needed Gospel in a broken dying world.

But did it happen?

So startling is this violent intrusion into the story that many scholars have questioned its historicity. If such a terrible event happened, they ask, why is there no mention of it in contemporary records? In particular, why does Josephus not mention it, when he is one of our most substantial sources for the excesses of Herod?

There can be little doubt that Matthew has present in his mind the parallels between Herod's massacre of children, and the story of Pharaoh's attempts to eliminate the Hebrew boys at birth in the Old Testament (Exodus 1:6-22). For Matthew this is an Old Testament parallel of significance. Just as Moses was saved from Pharaoh (ironically by Pharaoh's own daughter) to be the Saviour of his people, so Jesus was also saved from the hatred of a king to be the Saviour of his people. There are, however, differences that suggest that the Exodus story was not the source of his narrative, but a striking and illuminating parallel. Whereas the royal decree in ancient Egypt concerned newborn baby boys, Herod's soldiers were seeking for all boys under two years, as indicated by the story Herod had heard from the Magi.

More significant, however, is the well-documented paranoid fear, mistrust and violence of Herod in his later years. The massacre of children in Bethlehem, whilst an extreme reaction on Herod's part, is not at all out of character with his behaviour towards the end of his life. Early in his reign Herod had eliminated many of the Hasmonean family, who had preceded him in power. Amongst many other assassinations, he murdered Mariamne, his favourite wife, as well as a number of his own sons and close relatives[xxxv]. Characteristically when courtiers were executed for suspected disloyalty their entire families were killed with them. Allegedly he planned that, upon his death, a great number of Jewish leaders and nobility would be assembled in a stadium and slaughtered, to ensure that at least some people mourned when he died. In such an atmosphere of fear, mistrust and violence the murder of a handful of infants in the little village of Bethlehem would not be unlikely or out of character. Guides in Bethlehem will show you the exact graves in which the infant bodies were laid but that perhaps need not be taken too seriously!

Christian tradition has, of course, inflated the number of Herod's victims. The Byzantine liturgy records 14,000 "Holy Innocents". The Syrian Church acknowledges 64,000, and other estimates reach as high as 144,000 – echoing Revelation 14:1-4, where that is the number of the pure, who have not defiled themselves with women ("a safely attributed virtue at the age of two" as Raymond Brown comments[xxxvi]).

More realistically, the population of Bethlehem in the 1st century has been estimated at around 1000. Even allowing for the surrounding areas (vs.16), the number of boys of two years and under may have been more in the region of 20. This does not make the event any less appalling or the grief of the mothers that Matthew so poignantly records (vs.18) any less distressing. But an event on such a scale in the 1st century, particularly in Herod's world, would not necessarily have caused widespread shock.

For Matthew, however, this savage outbreak of violence, aimed at the Messiah, highlights the issues as the divine initiative for the salvation of the world begins to unfold. The Magi coming from the East have signalled the universal scope of God's love and invitation. His grace reaches even such boundaries. Herod, on the other hand, demonstrates the depravity and inhumanity that prevail when God's Word and his grace are rejected. The Magi seek the young king out to worship him.

Herod seeks him out to destroy him. Such is the choice before us all. A deadly conflict is underway – a divine humility shown in grace and sacrificial love confronting the demonic forces of death and inhumanity. Christ has not come for the improvement of the human race. He has come to save it from self inflicted destruction.

The Herod Question

But what shall we make of Herod, the villain of the piece? Do we just bracket him off, with Hitler, Stalin, Pol Pot and all the other hideous tyrants of history – demonize him, dehumanize him, and safely distance him from our own souls, our own temptations and dark places? This story needs to be read existentially[xxxvii]. It is not only the story of Persian Magi at the height of the Roman Empire finding their way to the feet of the Child Jesus in a modest home in Bethlehem. It is the story of how all of us can find our way to worship him, and the temptations along the way.

The Magi portray for us God's immense and immeasurable grace towards all of us who were once "without hope and without God in the world" and their story describes how we "who once were far away have been brought near" (Ephesians 2:12-13). In the same way Herod demonstrates for us how such a gracious invitation can go disastrously wrong. "Herod is an example of what can happen to us when we despise grace, no matter how far in or up we are"[xxxviii]. Herod heard the invitation to go to Bethlehem along with the Magi, but in him the invitation stirred up resistance, rejection and defensiveness. The result was that innocents around him were hurt as well. Sin is not only personal, it has social outworkings. It can be so with us too. We may count ourselves within the "people of God" but still possess Herod's heart of resistance and fear.

Rachel's Tears

Matthew's account of the brutal events in Bethlehem concludes with the second quotation from the Old Testament included in this chapter. The first had been the quotation produced by Herod's priestly advisors that the Christ would be born in Bethlehem (Micah 5:2 & Matt 2:6). The other two – this one and the reference to Jesus as a Nazarene (vs. 23) - are more problematic with regard to Matthew's intent.

The quotation here is undoubtedly hauntingly beautiful, tender - and painful:

> A voice is heard in Ramah,
> weeping and great mourning,
> Rachel weeping for her children
> and refusing to be comforted,
> because they are no more.

The quotation comes from Jeremiah, chapter 31: 15. Jeremiah is combining the memory of Rachel's sad death in childbirth "on the way to Bethlehem" (Gen. 35: 16-18) with the thought of her grieving from beyond the grave. Rachel was Jacob's favoured wife, "the mother of all Israel". Jeremiah uses this iconic moment of grief in Israel's history to describe the grief of the Jews as many of their number went into exile. They had been assembled at Ramah for the long march to Babylon. Today the site traditionally understood to be Rachel's tomb is just outside Bethlehem. Its inclusion in Israeli-controlled land necessitated a special loop of the Wall of Separation into Bethlehem territory. Rachel's death continues to be a source of grief in the Holy land today.

However, in Jeremiah's prophecy, the expression of grief and loss at Judah's brightest and best trudging into exile in Babylon, actually flows into an expression of hope in the following verses (vv. 16-17). . . . "Restrain your voice from weeping. . . your work will be rewarded. . . they will return. . . there is hope for your future. . . your children will return. . ."

Did Matthew intend this quotation to be a word of hope, that the death of the Bethlehem children would not be fruitless? Is it intended as an assurance that there would be future generations who would see the salvation brought by Emmanuel, the Child of Bethlehem whose birth had unleashed such grief? If so, why did he not continue the quotation? It appears that the grief and loss are the connection for Matthew.

He stared out on a nation devastated by Roman retribution visited against a rebellious people. He was writing his Gospel in a context where Jewish communities had been scattered, where the men folk had been crucified in their thousands. There was no immediate or easy comfort to be found, no quick fix. But nonetheless the God-with-us Saviour had been born and his universal message was bringing life into the destruction. Despite the hope-laden verses that follow it, Matthew's use here of the Jeremiah reference appears to be one principally of lament – an honest crying out to God in the face of unbearable pain and sorrow. The People of God are one community stretching across the whole span of human history. In Jeremiah's eyes the long-buried Rachel weeps over the exile of her children to Babylon

(597-587 BC), and in Matthew's eyes she now weeps over the slaughter of innocent children in Bethlehem (5 BC). And we might say, she weeps today over Bethlehem's children, over Syrian and Iraqi children, over Sudanese children, over children in Rotherham or Oxford, over all those orphaned by the violence generated by fear, greed and lust.

Christmas Lament

This is a moment in Matthew's account and in our annual retelling of the Christmas story that we dare not ignore. The Church's calendar instructs us to pay attention just a few days after our Christmas celebration. It ensures that our Christmas celebration is not just a welcome festival in the midst of winter, or an opportunity to spoil the children. It ensures that there are soldiers as well as angels. Herod is no pantomime villain, but the personification of the heartless, self-seeking, callous forces that always seek to eliminate the seemingly naive hopefulness of "peace on earth" proclaimed by the Babe in the manger. This event in our Christmas story calls us relentlessly to the exhilarating and the profoundly comforting reality of incarnation.

The birth of Jesus Christ is a birth as a full human being into the world as it really is; a world of extraordinary wonder and celebration, a world of inexplicable grief and loss. All of it. Only a God who enters all of it, who shares our life totally, who laughs and weeps with us, can know us, heal us and redeem us.

Ken Bailey's sharply-phrased comment bears repetition: "Why did Matthew think it important to record this unspeakably brutal act? Was it because love had an inexpressible incarnation at the same time and in the same place?"

The return from Egypt; James Tissot; Brooklyn Museum, NY

CHAPTER 9

HOME BY ANOTHER WAY

Matthew, chapter 2:

> **19** After Herod died, an angel of the Lord appeared in a dream to Joseph in Egypt **20** and said, "Get up, take the child and his mother and go to the land of Israel, for those who were trying to take the child's life are dead."
>
> **21** So he got up, took the child and his mother and went to the land of Israel. **22** But when he heard that Archelaus was reigning in Judea in place of his father Herod, he was afraid to go there. Having been warned in a dream, he withdrew to the district of Galilee, **23** and he went and lived in a town called Nazareth. So was fulfilled what was said through the prophets, "He will be called a Nazarene."

Perennial Problem

Into Egypt,
Joseph was sold,
rose to the heights,
and saved my people.

Out of Egypt,
Moses was freed,
received my Law,
and led my people.

Out of Egypt,
I called my Son,
brought by family,
renewing my people.

Sepphoris

To stand on the steep ruin-clad hill of Sepphoris is to gain a wholly new understanding of the nature of ancient Galilee. The assumption that Galilee was a quiet rural backwater where Jesus grew up in a peaceful Jewish community, and was formed by quiet reflection on countryside and lake seeps away as you stand there. This is "Galilee of the Gentiles" – indeed well-populated by Jews

> Threat of death passed over,
> bypassing Judea,
> Galilee beckons,
> Nazareth welcomes,
> my Refugee.
>
> Tragically, later,
> home town rejects
> home grown Prophet,
> who cites my acts
> for people outside.
>
> Unsightly reaction incited:
> my perennial problem.

since the time of the Hasmonean rulers (Judas Maccabaeus and his family), but also a major trading thoroughfare, from the Mediterranean Sea through to Lake Galilee, the Greek cities of the Decapolis on the lake's eastern shore, and the cities of Syria, Mesopotamia and the Persian Empire. It was agriculturally fertile, commercially prosperous and a desirable home for Greeks, Romans, Egyptians, easterners from Mesopotamia and Persia as well as Jewish settlers from further south.

The hill of Sepphoris stands overlooking this strategic thoroughfare of the ancient world. Herod seized the hill-top stronghold early in his reign (37BC) and fortified it as his northern headquarters which it remained throughout his reign. At his death his family temporarily lost control of the city until Herod Antipas regained it and used as his capital as ruler of Galilee until he moved his residence to Tiberias on the lake. Antipas rebuilt and developed the site until it became what Josephus called "the jewel of all Galilee" and the "strongest city in Galilee." It was renowned for its splendour. It was less than 4 miles from Nazareth.

Home by Another Way

News of Herod's death (4BC) would have reached Joseph in Egypt very quickly. For the third time (1:20-21, 2:13, 2:19-20) Joseph is guided in a dream to care for and to protect his precious young family. Not just Herod, but others of his counsellors who would wish the child harm, have died. Here, again, the parallel with the story of Moses is underlined. Moses, in exile in Sinai, had also been assured that "all the men who wanted to kill you are dead" (Ex 4:19).

Just as in Bethlehem he had got up to flee south to Egypt into safety, now he got up to bring his family home. But where is home? Bethlehem, with its association with King David, is clearly unsafe, as is Jerusalem, home of so much biblical promise. Herod may have died but his similarly capricious and murderous son, Archelaus, is on the throne and an equal threat. Archelaus "inherited his father's unpopularity without his political skill"[xxxix]. In 6AD he was deposed by Rome following complaints of his "cruelty and tyranny". Thereafter Judea and Samaria were ruled directly by a Roman prefect. At the time of Jesus' ministry this was Pontius Pilate (AD26-36). Galilee continued to be ruled by Herod's son Antipas, famously the murderer of John the Baptist, and branded by Jesus as "that fox."

Reaching Judah and the region of Bethlehem and Jerusalem, doubtless already anxious, Joseph was further warned in a dream, and travelled further north with his family to an obscure little village in Galilee, known as Nazareth.

Nazareth had the advantage of almost total obscurity and that was what Joseph was seeking. He had had enough of politics and intrigue and wanted security for his family. Nazareth had no history. It was not mentioned in the Old Testament. It was probably founded little more than a hundred years previously, as a "new town" for migrants from Judah. Nathanael, when invited to become a disciple of Jesus, and himself a native of nearby Cana, said, "Can anything good come out of Nazareth?" (John 1:46)

Apart from his dream, and apart from earlier family connections (referred to in Luke's Gospel), Joseph may have had good reason for basing himself in Nazareth. Just over the hill was Sepphoris, with an extensive building programme that continued throughout Jesus' childhood and early adulthood. Though we have no way of knowing, there is the possibility that Joseph worked as a carpenter / master builder at Sepphoris throughout Jesus' upbringing, and that perhaps Jesus himself worked there in the family business.

Nazareth has become a large town. Its association with the childhood of Jesus sustains the tourist trade, but time and economic development have largely built over, obliterated or simply lost the ancient settlement. Sepphoris on the other hand offers some startling moments of connection with the story of Jesus. There can be no doubt that this was a town that Jesus knew well, and where he may well have worked. Its surviving streets are very likely aligned just as Jesus would have known them. From one vantage point you can look out over a large market area, perhaps 20-30 metres across. It has a largely complete mosaic floor. The nearer part is decorated with animal motifs, and is later than the first century. The area beyond has geometrical designs, perhaps reflecting a Jewish objection to artistic representation, and is confidently dated to the first century. As you stand at that vantage point you are possibly looking at a market floor on which Jesus himself walked, perhaps haggling for the family's supplies. It is a moment of strange and powerful connection with the story and life experience of Jesus.

A Messiah from Nazareth?

Matthew seems to be unaware of the tradition, known to Luke, that the family's roots were in Nazareth (Luke 1:26 ff.) However he is well aware of Jesus' upbringing in Nazareth – and that this creates a challenge. Can "Jesus of *Nazareth*" (of all places) be the awaited Messiah?

In his rich multilayered introduction to his Gospel (chs 1 & 2) he has demonstrated how Jesus' lineage identifies him as both the Son of Abraham and the Son of David. In his naming he is proclaimed as Jesus the Saviour, and Emmanuel, God with us. The story of the Magi demonstrates how the promise to Abraham that through him all the people of the earth will be blessed works out, as these strange figures come to worship the Child. And in the story of the flight into Egypt and the massacre of infant boys in Bethlehem, a radically new and provocative understanding of Messiahship emerges, of God being with us in the world. Thus the task is almost done: Jesus' origins are rooted in Bethlehem and in the promises to Abraham and David. But how can the man, commonly known as "Jesus of Nazareth", be the Messiah?

> When Jesus entered Jerusalem, the whole city was stirred and asked, "Who is this?" The crowds answered, "This is Jesus, the prophet from Nazareth in Galilee."
>
> (Matt 21:10-11)

Matthew's answer is contained in verse 23:

> So (Joseph) went and lived in a town called Nazareth. So was fulfilled what was said through the prophets, "He will be called a Nazarene."

Matthew's intention is to demonstrate that the Messiah can indeed be a citizen of Nazareth. That Jesus of Nazareth is the Messiah from Bethlehem. There are, however, several tricky problems with his explanation, which despite much scholarly endeavour have never been very satisfactorily resolved. First, Nazareth did not exist in Old Testament times, so no prophet would have been able to refer to such a place. And secondly, nowhere in the Old Testament, or indeed in other contemporary literature, can such a quote be found. Somehow we still miss the connections that Matthew intended his readers to make.

There is no need here to follow the scholarly discussion in detail, except perhaps just to become aware of a contribution by the commentator R T France. France takes as his starting point the reality that Nazareth is, from every perspective, a "nowhere place", a derogatory name-calling kind of place. This would connect Jesus with the "humble Messiah" passage in the Old Testament (especially Isaiah 53 –" one despised and rejected") rather than the "royal Messiah" passages. The view that the Messiah could be an incognito kind of figure was current in New Testament times: "When the Messiah comes, no-one knows where he comes from"[xl].

On this view, Matthew's depiction of the man from Nazareth as the Messiah is a reminder of the Old Testament tradition that no one will know where the Messiah comes from.

This Messiah comes from the wrong place and does the wrong things. He will be rejected and despised. He will lay down his life for his people.[xli] This would be in harmony with the fact that we know that Jesus distanced himself from the accepted Messianic language, preferring the more ambiguous term "Son of Man".

It is interesting to note that already by the middle of the 1st century, Christians were sometimes called Nazarenes (*nazaraios*) in a derogatory sense (Acts 24:5). In Syria and in other parts of the Muslim world for many centuries it has also been common, and indeed in a derogatory sense, to call Christians *nasraya* or *nasara.* Today in a more sinister way, the Arabic letter "nun" (more or less identical with the English letter "n") has been daubed on Christian homes in Mosul and other towns in Iraq and Syria to mark them out as targets in any future action against Christians.

"He will be called a Nazarene" (Matt 2:23). And so he was. And so were his followers, then and also today. It is a sign of vulnerability and humility. We are Christians, and also Nazarenes.

Jesus of Nazareth is the Messiah of Bethlehem

The Magi returned home "by another way". Christian tradition and possibly Matthew himself intended us to understand that they returned home changed and reorientated, the tools of their trade consecrated to new uses. In his careful story-telling, Matthew concludes the second phase of his narrative with the home-coming of the Messiah, also by an unexpected route, dictated, like the Magi, by fear of Herod's dangerous family.

On one level the return to Nazareth in Galilee was a journey in search of safety and security, of obscurity. On another level, Joseph was providing for his family, locating himself at the heart of a cosmopolitan, thriving community, culturally, religiously and linguistically complex, where there would be work for a skilled carpenter. As Jesus grew, we can imagine him growing in the life of the local synagogue, perhaps walking to Sepphoris with his father for work or to visit the market. He would not have mixed much with the communities he found there, but he would have been aware of the urban lifestyles, the theatre and baths, the gulf between the rich and powerful, and the poor and weak, the different cultures and religious practices, the different languages. He would have been aware of the trade links to the west, to Egypt, Greece and Rome, and to the east, to the Decapolis, Syria, Mesopotamia and beyond.

In such a world his identity began to form, his awareness that he must be about his Father's business. His understanding of the meaning and implications of the ancient covenants of Israel's God with Abraham and with David would have slowly matured within him, until the day when. . .

> Jesus went into Galilee, proclaiming the good news of God. "The time has come", he said, "The kingdom of God is near. Repent and believe the good news."
>
> (Mark 1:14-15)

Adoration of the Magi; Unknown

The Church and the Nations

God the Father forms his people,
from out of the nations to bless the nations;
Jesus the Christ saves his people,
from out of the nations to bless the nations;
The Holy Spirit draws his people,
from out of the nations to bless the nations.
Abraham called,
from out of the nations, the people are blessed;
Moses leads,
from out of a nation, a people oppressed;
David fights,
against the nations, the people assured;
Isaiah speaks,
to lighten the nations, the people restored.
Jesus dies,
betrayed by the people, for the people;
Jesus dies,
pierced by the nations, for the nations.
Jesus raised,
the people remade, the nations reproached;
Paul proclaims,
the people reshaped, the nations rejoice;
John sees,
the people redeemed, regathered from every tribe, tongue, people and nation.

CHAPTER 10

Desire of Nations

The Longing of Humanity

> Sages, leave your contemplations;
> Brighter visions beam afar;
> Seek the great Desire of Nations;
> Ye have seen his natal star!
> (James Montgomery, 'Angels from the Realms of Glory')

James Montgomery's familiar Christmas carol picks up the Old Testament reference from the prophet Haggai and links it appropriately with the "sages" following the star. Charles Wesley did the same in a verse of "Hark the Herald Angels Sing" which we rarely sing nowadays:

> Come, Desire of nations, come.
> Fix in us thy humble home.

Haggai lived in Judah as the survivors of exile in Babylon were straggling home in the mid 6th century BC, and he was attempting to connect them with their historic sense of identity and calling.

The writings that make up our Old and New Testaments, emerging from Israel's and early Christian history, weave together an extraordinary vision not just for the communities that produced them, but for all the nations of the earth. To take on board just what is being said, then and now, is to have your world view radically changed – so that it truly becomes a *world* view. The seeds of this strange and unique journey were sown as the Creator God in Genesis 12 and subsequent chapters, out of love for all the human race, chose one man, Abraham, to carry his purposes forward. He was hardly promising material as he and his wife were already well past child-bearing age. Nonetheless, the God who speaks to us through these scriptures chose to bless Abraham and Sarah's family, as yet unborn, and through them to bless all the nations of the world.

At no time in Israel's history was she a "great nation", and yet this double-sided theme was never lost. It was debated and dialogued with. At times its more inward and nationalist dimension was emphasised and the openness to the wider world lost. At other times the drawing in of all the nations shone out clearly.

In the wake of the Exile, as the returnees struggled to rebuild nation, city and Temple out of the rubble, vision was in short supply. Haggai attempted to lift the eyes of the people to the high and wide nature of their national calling. Remember, he was saying, it is so much more than what you can see at present.

> This is what the LORD Almighty says, ". . . I will shake all nations, and the desired of all nations shall come, and I will fill this house with glory."
>
> (Haggai 2:6-7)

The translation and interpretation of the phrase "desired (or Desire) of nations" is not straightforward, but Haggai's intention is to place Judah's journey at this point in her history once again in the context of God's purpose of blessing both for Israel and for the nations. Was it intended to be a reference to God's coming Messiah? Many scholars are uncertain, but the phrase "Desire of Nations" has resounded down the centuries as capturing the significance of Jesus as the one in whom the ancient promise of blessing is fulfilled, in whom the desires and longings of the nations and of the human race are satisfied. James Montgomery and Charles Wesley, two of our great hymn writers, use the phrase with just that intent. And John, the writer of Revelation, captures its eventual realisation in the conclusion to his book, and the conclusion to our Bible:

> The city (the new Jerusalem) does not need the sun or moon to shine on it, for the glory of God gives it light and the Lamb is its lamp. The nations will walk by its light, and the kings of the earth will bring their splendour into it. . . The glory and honour of the nations will be brought into it.
>
> (Revelation 21: 23-26)

Worship and Witness

For Matthew, the story of the Magi making their pilgrimage from the far-off pagan East to worship Christ captures the ancient longing of Israel's scriptures that she would be the vehicle by which God's promise of blessing to all the nations would be realised. As the Son of Abraham, Christ is the bearer of the Promise to the nations. As the Son of David, he can rightfully receive the worship of these envoys of the nations. As Emmanuel he is the living presence of God amongst his people and the one through whom this Promise would now be carried throughout the world. The Desire of the Nations had come.

As we have clearly seen, this opening narrative of Matthew's Gospel is no mere colourful prologue. It is the "Gospel in miniature" in which many of the key themes of worship, witness, faith, conflict and discipleship emerge.

Two of these – Worship and Witness – are particularly important to Matthew. They are, as it were, the bookends of his Gospel. In the story of the Magi, the heart of the story, is the moment at which the Magi bow in worship and offer their gifts to the new born King. From that moment the dynamic of witness and mission is released. The violence of those who hate the Child is unleashed, the Magi return home transformed, by another" Way", and the flight of the Holy Family into Egypt establishes their identification with the poor and displaced and the strange reversals that characterise missionary purpose.

These same themes shape the conclusion of the Gospel in chapter 28. Following the resurrection on Easter morning, Christ meets Mary Magdalene and the "other Mary", mother of James and John (28:9). They clasp his feet and worship him – and are immediately commissioned to tell "his brothers" to go to Galilee where they will meet him. Worship leads on immediately to sharing the news of the Resurrected Lord.

> Can the church's doctrine of the two natures be put more succinctly? They "grabbed his *feet*" – he is a human being! They *worshipped* him – he is God! [xlii]

To worship *Jesus,* is totally to have acknowledged that he is God-with-us, and that we need go nowhere else. "To whom else shall we go? You have the words of eternal life" (John 6:68). We do not worship him as well as, or instead of, God the Father.

We have come to see that in Jesus we connect with God in our humanity, that he is God, extended down to where we are.

Later, in Galilee, the disciples met Christ as they had been promised. "When they saw him they worshipped him; but some doubted." Immediately, the Risen Lord gave his missionary commission to the disciples, a commission to "all nations", picking up the Abraham theme :

> "All authority in heaven and on earth is given to me. Therefore go and make disciples of all nations, baptising them in the name of the Father, and of the Son, and of the Holy Spirit, and teaching them to obey everything I have commanded you. And surely I am with you always, to the very end of the age."
>
> (Matthew 28:16-20)

The reference in the Great Commission to "all nations" creates the Church's world vision. After this, Christians can no longer be tribal, local, or parochial. We are intoxicated with the possibility that the Gospel can reach the ends of the earth. "The world is my parish", said John Wesley. "Christians are now hopelessly, incurably missionary and evangelistic" [xliii] says the commentator Frederick Bruner.

Matthew's view of the essentials of Christian discipleship and community are plain. The heart of faithful Christian living is the constant interplay of Worship and Witness, Worship and Mission. Our attention, individually and corporately, needs to be constantly moving from the worship of Christ to the sharing of the Good News in word and deed, and back again. Only lives touched, cleansed, forgiven, renewed by worshipping at his feet, only lives poured out as a gift for him, can live in the world another way, witnessing to him who is, though unrecognised, the Desire of Nations.

We have passed over two significant little phrases. When the disciples worshipped the Risen Lord, "some doubted." This phrase rather jars with us as we absorb Matthew's final verses. "Some doubted". Why? Why now? Some translators have suggested "hesitated" might be better. But there can be little doubt that Matthew meant "doubt". In his Gospel, as well as in the other Synoptic Gospels, the doubt of the disciples emerges repeatedly (see, for example, Matt 14:31 & 21:21). It would have been easy to remove this element from the Gospels, to present the disciples as models of faith. But our gospel writers know that doubt and uncertainty are experiences we all have in our lives of discipleship. There is no doubt-free discipleship. Do we, then, have to wait to be in some more perfect condition of faith before we can participate in Christ's mission? Absolutely not. It is disciples who are both believing and doubting who are called and commissioned to go into all the world and make disciples. It is *as we go* that we experience the presence of the Risen Christ, the one who has promised to be with us until the very end of the age. It is *as we go* that we experience the truth of the Gospel and see it at work in our lives, the lives of those we meet, and in the world. The inclusiveness of the Gospel is not only about all the diversity of languages and cultures in the world, but also all our diversities of faith and understanding, of gift and motivation. As Albert Schweitzer said, "Follow him and you will know him."

The second phrase is the very conclusion of the Gospel: "And surely I am with you always to the very end of the age" (28:20) Here is another "bookend" for Matthew's Gospel. Immediately following his account of the birth of Jesus in Chapter 1, Matthew introduces him to us as "Immanuel" – God with us. Throughout the Gospel it is plain that he means more than a general assurance of the presence of God. He means very specifically that God is present with us, in the here and now, in the very precise human presence of Jesus. And he concludes his Gospel with an Immanuel assurance from Jesus. "Here and now, every day, in your worship and your witness, from now until the end of time I am with you, I am Immanuel."

The experience of Jesus being with us, in and through each other, is very important for Matthew – for him "Immanuel" is a present ongoing reality. "He who receives you receives me, and he who receives me receives the one who sent me," says Jesus (10:40) and again (18:20) "For where two or three come together in my name, there I am with them." And, of course, the so-called parable of the sheep and goats teaches us that whenever we feed the hungry, clothe the naked and visit the sick or those in prison, we do it to and for him.

With the "God-with-us Saviour" into Mission today

And what is Matthew saying to the Church today about our calling into the world through the strange visitors from the east? Here, I believe, are some of the challenges:

i. We need to dismantle our instinctive social, cultural and national narrowness and embrace the radically inclusive nature of God's call to come to worship Christ. The communities that result will often be very diverse.

ii. We need to welcome the "strangeness" and the diversity of ways in which people find their way to Christ.

The desire to find the one "born King of the Jews" arises in many different and surprising contexts of cultural ferment. For example, alongside the destructive hatreds running amok in many parts of the Middle East many remarkable movements to Christian Faith can be identified.

iii. God speaks and calls people to begin the journey to faith in Jesus through cultural and religious frameworks that are often very alien to the Biblical worldview. But only the scriptural testimony to Christ can in the end make the encounter true and transforming.

iv. The journey to find Christ and to worship him is often a long pilgrimage, with long stretches without a "star to guide" and with dangerous encounters along the way.

v. The encounter with Jesus leads to worship – worship of him as the one in whom the promise of God to all the nations is made present and brought to fulfilment. He is the Desire of Nations, and Immanuel, the "God-with-us Saviour."

vi. The encounter with Jesus in worship is transforming and sends us home to our own culture and world, but transformed, and "by another way." This is how worship flows into witness that is personal, characterised by testimony, and engaged with our context and culture.

vii. WORSHIP and MISSION are the twin poles of authentic Christian living. We need continually to reflect on how our worship of Christ can lead us into mission and witness to Christ, and how our mission can lead us back into worship.

viii. The blessing of the nations that has been made actual in Christ and in his death and resurrection, is a real blessing in the social, political, personal and cultural life of humanity. It is incarnate in the earthy realities of human life. It is marked by an identification with the poor, the displaced, the vulnerable and the needy, rather than with the powerful. Immanuel is found in the person of the Child fleeing down the roads to Egypt, not in the palaces of Jerusalem.

I offer these tentatively, arising from an extended reflection on Matthew's startling opening story. Interpreted into his own cultural and historical context, would he recognise them as in any way capturing his own convictions about the significance of Christ? Given the "game-changing" significance of the Antioch Church (if that was Matthew's home community) in the story of Christian cross-cultural mission, would they recognise these themes as their heritage?

And how might local church life, practice and mission today be changed if we endeavoured to live in the light of the strange story of the Child, the Magi, Herod, the butchered children of Bethlehem and the refugee family fleeing through the desert to Egypt?

> The question is not whether either the heritage of Western Christianity or the emergence of non-Western Christianity is "right" or "wrong". The young Christians in Antioch never questioned whether the faith of the church in Jerusalem was true. Rather, the question was, and is, whether the Spirit continues to be at work whenever the Gospel crosses cultural, social and geographical boundaries, expanding the reach of God's love, and becoming incarnate again in his body.
> (Wesley Granberg-Michaelson From Times Square to Timbuktu) [xliv]

And what on earth happened to the Magi when they reached home?

Source of the Church,
Desire of the nations;
Head of the Church,
Judge of the nations;
Breath of the Church,
Light of the nations;
Father, Son and Holy Spirit,
renew your Church to bless your nations.

Picture by Robin Wainwright

Bibliography

These books have been particularly helpful in my journey with the Magi.

Anderson, Allan Heaton To the Ends of the Earth. Pentecostalism and the Transformation of World Christianity Oxford, 2013

Ateek, Naim Stifan A Palestinian Christian Cry for Reconciliation Orbis, New York, 2008

Ateek, Naim et al. eds Challenging Empire. God, Faithfulness and Resistance Jerusalem 2012

Bailey, Kenneth E Jesus Through Middle Eastern Eyes. Cultural Studies in the Gospels SPCK, London, 2008

Bauckham, Richard Jesus and the God of Israel Paternoster 2008

Brown, Raymond E The Birth of the Messiah. A Commentary on the Infancy Narratives in the Gospels of Matthew and Luke, updated edition, Yale, 1993

Bruner, Frederick Dale Matthew A Commentary. Vol.1 The Christbook. Matthew 1-12. Revised and Expanded Edition, Grand Rapids , 2007

Cowan, James Fleeing Herod. A Journey Through Coptic Egypt with the Holy Family. Massachusetts, 2013.)

France, R T The Gospel of Matthew New International Commentary of the New Testament, Grand Rapids, 2007

Granberg-Michaelson, Wesley From Times Square to Timbuctu. The Post-Christian West Meets the Non-Western Church Grand Rapids, 2013

Green, Michael The Message of Matthew The Bible Speaks Today Series, IVP 2000

Montefiore, Simon Sebag Jerusalem. The Biography London, 2011

Morley, Janet Haphazard by Starlight. A Poem a Day from Advent to Epiphany SPCK, 2013

Murphy O'Connor, Jerome The Holy Land. An Oxford Archaeological Guide , Oxford , 5th edition 2008

Peskett, Howard & Ramachandra, Vinoth The Message of Mission The Bible Speaks Today Series, IVP, 2003

Powell, Mark Allan, Chasing the Eastern Star. Adventures in Biblical Reader-Response Criticism, John Knox Press, Louisville, 2001

Raheb, Mitri Faith in the Face of Empire. The Bible Through Palestinian Eyes 2014

Russell, Gerard Heirs to Forgotten Kingdoms. Journeys into the Disappearing Religions of the Middle East. Simon & Schuster, London, 2014.

Sanneh, Lamin Disciples of All Nations. Pillars of World Christianity Oxford 2008

Smith. David Mission After Christendom, Darton, Longman & Todd, 2003

Smith, David The Kindness of God. Christian Witness in Our Troubled World, IVP , 2013

Steven, Kenneth C Iona. Poems Edinburgh, 2000

Taylor, John V The Christlike God SCM, London, 1992

Tickle, Phyllis Emergence Christianity. What it is, Where it is going and Why it matters Grand Rapids, , 2012

Wheeler, Andrew Bombs, Ruins and Honey. Journeys of the Spirit with Sudanese Christians Nairobi, 2006

Yamauchi, Edwin M Persia and the Bible, Grand Rapids, 1996

Personal notes

Personal notes

ENDNOTES

---

[i] Andrew Walls, "The Ephesian Moment" in The Cross-Cultural Process in Christian History, Edinburgh, 2002, p.78

[ii] Michael Green The Message of Matthew The Bible Speaks Today Series. Revised edition 2000, IVP p. 68

[iii] Personal experience.

[iv] Raymond Brown The Birth of the Messiah. A Commentary on the Infancy Narratives in the Gospels of Matthew and Luke, Anchor Yale Bible ,1993, p. 174 (Updated Edition)

[v] These are: Matt 1:23, 2:6, 2:15, 2:18 & 2:23

[vi] Bruner, op.cit. p.61

[vii] The classic biography of Kivebulaya is by Anne Luck

[viii] Quoted in Bruner Commentary p. 65.

[ix] Bruner op.cit. Vol. 1 pp. 65-73

[x] Aramaic is still used as a liturgical language (commonly termed Syriac) in many Eastern Churches, i.e. The Assyrian Churches, the Thomas Churches in India, the Syrian orthodox Church and others.

[xi] The whole poem is called BC:AD and plays with the sense of Before and After that the Christmas story suggests. It can be found in Janet Morley Haphazard by Starlight. A Poem a Day from Advent to Epiphany. SPCK 2013, p.90. It was originally published in a volume of New and Collected Poems, edited by R.V. Bailey in 2010

[xii] Brown, Raymond. The Birth of the Messiah p.183

[xiii] Not to be confused with Caesarea Philippi, close to Mount Hermon, and scene of Peter's confession of Jesus as the Messiah. This was also largely constructed by Herod, with a large temple to the Greek god Pan.

[xiv] Dawson W. Carr Andrew Mantegna. The Adoration of the Magi. Getty Museum Studies on Art, Los Angeles, 1997 is an excellent discussion of the painting which I have used extensively.

[xv] Carr pp. 88-9.

[xvi] I recall reading an exposition of this passage by St Chrysostom along these lines but cannot now find it.

[xvii] Save the Children and UNHCR websites October 2013

[xviii] Acts 8:26

[xix] Edward Shillitoe (1872-1948) was a Free Church minister in England during the First World War

[xx] John V Taylor The Christlike God London, 1992, p.196.

[xxi] France op.cit. p.79, quoting Philo.

[xxii][xxii] France op.cit. p. 77

[xxiii] This story is told more fully in Wheeler, Andrew Bombs, Ruins and Honey Paulines Press, Nairobi, 2006, pp. 91 - 106

[xxiv] For these Old Testament parallels see France op.cit. pp.77-79, and Brown, op.cit. pp.214-6.

[xxv] Bruner op.cit. p. 73

[xxvi] Egypt was initially conquered by Arab armies under Amr bin al'As in 642AD

[xxvii] John 11.

[xxviii] James Cowan set out to travel Egypt in the footsteps of the Holy Family, and his lively and at times dream like book relays many of the stories of the Holy Family in Egypt (Cowan, James Fleeing Herod. A Journey Through Coptic Egypt with the Holy Family. Massachusetts, 2013.)

[xxix] Luke 23: 32-43

[xxx] Matt 28: 19-20

[xxxi] Bruner, Frederick Dale. Matthew: A Commentary Vol. 1. P.68.

[xxxii] This story, describing one of the very formative events of the second civil war in S Sudan (1983-2005) is told in greater length in Werner, Anderson & Wheeler Day of Devastation, Day of Contentment. The History of the Sudanese Church Across 2000 years Second Edition, Nairobi, pp. 394-400.

[xxxiii] Op.cit. p. 68

[xxxiv] Cited in Bruner, p.69. Bailey was writing in *The Presbyterian Outlook* for December 2001

[xxxv] Caesar Augustus joked that "it is better to be Herod's pig than his son."

[xxxvi] Brown, Raymond E. The Birth of the Messiah p.205.

[xxxvii] "It is only when we learn to see ourselves in the problematic people of the Gospel – from the four questionable couples in the genealogy, through the Magi. . . and now Herod, to the Pharisees,, Romans, *and failing disciples* at the passion – that we will be reading the Gospel existentially. Herod is Original Sin and this Deep Sin lives on. . ." (Bruner, op.cit. p. 66)

[xxxviii] Bruner op.cit. p.69.

[xxxix] France, op.cit. p.90.

[xl] See the conflict in contemporary views represented in John 7: 27, & 7:42.

[xli] The scholarly discussion is complex. An accessible place to follow it up is France R T The Gospel of Matthew pp.91-95.

[xlii] Bruner op. cit. 796

[xliii] Op.cit. 817

[xliv] Granberg-Michaelson From Times Square to Timbuktu. The Post-Christian West Meets the Non-Western Church Eerdmans, 2013, p. 151